Delighting in the Feminine Divine

Bridget Mary Meehan

Illustrations by
Gloria Ortiz

Sheed & Ward

Sheed & Ward™ is a service of The National Catholic Reporter Publishing Company.

————————◆————————

Library of Congress Cataloguing-in-Publication Data

Meehan, Bridget.
    Delighting in the feminine divine / Bridget Mary Meehan ; illustrations by Gloria Ortiz.
      p.   cm.
    Includes bibliographical references.
    ISBN 1-55612-658-1 (alk. paper)
    1. Spiritual exercises. 2. Femininity of God--Prayer-
books and devotions--English. 3. Catholic Church--Prayer-
books and devotions--English. I. Title.
BX2182.2.M356   1994
231'.4--dc20   93-44593
                                               CIP

————————◆————————

Published by: Sheed & Ward
                  115 E. Armour Blvd.
                  P.O. Box 419492
                  Kansas City, MO 64141

To order, call: (800) 333-7373

Illustrations by Gloria Ortiz

Dedication

To my family: my parents, Bridie and Jack, my Aunt Molly McCarthy, my brothers Patrick and Sean, my sisters-in-law Valerie and Nancy, my niece and nephew Katie and Danny.

To all the women whose strength and compassion have reflected to me the love of God as Sister and Friend: especially Regina Madonna Oliver S.S.C., Mary Emma Haddrick S.S.C., Irene Marshall, Daisy Sullivan, Peg Bowen, Maria Billick, Elizabeth Hoisington, Doris Mason, Mary Cashman C.D.P., Roseanne Fedorko S.S.J., Mary Guertin, Rosemary Walsh I.H.M., Michael Morsches, Patricia Herlihy, Ana Minassian, Mary Patricia Mulhall, Evelyn Mulhall, Kathleen Mulhall, Mary and Megan Fitzgibbons, Kaye Brown, Anita McCowen, Sue Wenzel, Mary Jo Grotenrath, Estelle Spachman, Debbie Dubuque, Eileen Kelly P.B.V.M., Melanie Maczka, S.S.C. and the Society of Sisters for the Church.

To all Celtic Women in my family: Noreen Davy, Molly Meehan, Mary Ferns, Peg Meehan, Mary Tregent, Margaret Ryan, Mary D. Meehan, Eileen Meehan, Kathleen McNamara, Esther Meehan, Tess Murphy, Mary Meehan, Alice Meehan, Elizabeth Murphy, Catherine Murphy, Rose Meehan, Katherine Meehan, Miriam Meehan and Eileen Preston.

To Mary, Mother of Jesus and Mother of the Church, whose courageous discipleship and companionship reflects the liberating power of Sophia-God.

Acknowledgments

I am grateful to Regina Madonna Oliver S.S.C. who offered encouragement, support, keen insights, and editorial assistance in the writing of this book. I am deeply indebted to the women who participated in this adventure and shared their wisdom and experiences of delighting in the Feminine Divine in part four of this book: Regina Madonna Oliver S.S.C., Pat Lehrer, Nancy Long, Donna Mogan, Nanette Wisser M.S.C., Nancy M. Healy S.F.C.C., Bettie McNamara Fretz, The Sophia Group from Reading, Pa.— Maria Esterbrook, Renee J. Fox, Pamela Kubacki, Lynda Kuhn, Mary Lou Creyts, Theresa Molchanow, M.S.C. I am grateful also to Georgia Keightley for writing the preface to this book and to the artist Gloria Ortiz for her powerful illustrations. I owe special gratitude to Rev. Michael Pollitt for translating some of the medieval texts from Latin to English and to friends such as Fritz Warren, Bruce Burslie, Gene Razzetti, Ron Whalen, Larry Skummer, Dennis Wenzel, Jack Doyle, Rev. Frank Keefe, Rev. Joe Mulqueen, Rev. John Weyand, Mike Marshall, Bob Schaaf and Bob Bowen whose openness and encouragement have been wonderful gifts to me. Carol and Ray Buchanan provided expert advice on technical computer issues.

Contents

Preface, *Dr. Georgia Keightley* ix

Introduction xi

Part One
The Feminine Divine in the Hebrew Scriptures

A Hovering Nesting Mother Bird 5

Creating Human Life in Her Image 7

Sheltering Those in Difficulty under the Shadow of Her Wings 11

Eagle/Spirit Winging the Enslaved toward Freedom . . . 14

Shekinah: She-Who-Dwells-Within 16

Shekinah: Transforming the Church 18

El Shaddai: God the Breasted One 20

Humanity in the Womb of God 22

Washerwoman God 24

God as Seamstress 26

Part Two
The Feminine Divine in Sophia and Jesus-Sophia

Sophia: Angry Preacher 36

Sophia: Liberator 39

Sophia: Tree of Life and Mentor 43

Sophia: Welcoming Hostess 45

Sophia: Mother 49

Sophia: Crucified Christ 52

Jesus-*Sophia*: Healer of Our Stress 54

Women Prophets Persecuted 56

Jesus: Mirror of *Sophia* 58

Sophia: and the Woman Caught in Adultery 60

Part Three
The Feminine Divine in the Christian Tradition

Clement of Alexandria 65

God the Nourisher 66

John Chrysostom 67

Eucharist as Nourishment 68

Brigit of Kildare 71

    Mother Goddess and Christian Saint 73

Augustine of Hippo, Thomas Aquinas, Albert the Great,
and Julian of Norwich 76

    The Wisdom of God as Mother 78

Anselm of Canterbury 81

    Jesus as Mother 82

St. Bernard of Clairvaux 85

    Jesus as Mother and the Abbot as Mother 87

Mechtild von Hackeborn 90

    Mother God 91

Hildegard of Bingen 93

    A Vision of the Feminine Divine 95

Marguerite of Oingt 97

    Mother Jesus Birthing the World 98

Julian of Norwich 100

    The Wisdom of the Trinity as our Mother 102

    Merciful Mother Jesus 104

Part 4
Reflections of Contemporary Women

Ammah's Lullaby, *Regina Madonna Oliver* 108

Grandmother God, *Bettie McNamara Fretz* 111

Delighting in the Magic of the Feminine Divine, *Nancy Long* 114

Mother Eagle and the Reluctant Risk-Taker, *Nanette M. Wisser* 119

Mother God—Maker of the Beautiful, *Nanette M. Wisser* . 120

Wisdom as Playful Craftswoman, *Donna M. Mogan* . . . 122

The Fruits of God's Mother-Touch, *Pat Lehrer* 125

A Balloon Ride With Sophia, *Sophia Group* 128

Epiphany, *Nancy M. Healy* 131

The One Who Answers When I Call, *Regina Madonna Oliver* 133

Women—Images of the Feminine Divine, *Bridget Mary Meehan* 136

Resource Suggestions for Delighting in the Feminine Divine 139

Preface

It is a distinct pleasure to be invited to write the preface for the second of Bridget Mary Meehan's books on the subject of the divine feminine. That her first, *Exploring the Feminine Face of God*, was received with the excitement and enthusiasm it has really comes as no suprise. There is a great yearning today for the experience of God and for learning the ways to open up the everyday so that the spiritual in which we live, move and have our being, might be encountered in its fullness, in all its richness.

Like the book that preceded it, this one too presents and explores the many different references to the feminine in deity that enrich and proliferate the Christian tradition. Included here are the insights of scripture, of theologians like Clement of Alexandria, John Chrysostom, Anselm of Canterbury, Hildegard of Bingen, of such visionaries as Mechtild von Hackeborn, Marguerite of Oingt. But at the same time that a careful retrieval of the materials available to us in scripture and tradition is made, the book concludes with some creative new efforts to express God's feminine depths. *Ammah's Lullabye* is an especially powerful, meaningful example of this, as is the author's own poetic summary of images.

In this text one is presented not just an opportunity to appreciate and learn from the feminine in God. More importantly, the reader is allowed both the freedom to accept, the freedom to affirm those human traits and values that western culture has traditionally identified with woman.

Steadfast, uncompromising love and fidelity, patience, gentleness, the tasks of healer, welcoming hostess, birth giver, devoted parent and tireless nurturer—all of these are things that have long been considered by patriarchal society as being inferior and betraying weakness. Yet in being identified with God's own nature, these attributes and works are affirmed here not only for their exquisite humanness. They are also presented as being expressive of, as pertaining to the divine's own essence. Thus they become something to celebrate, something to value and treasure.

Perhaps the aspect the reader will appreciate most are the exercises for reflection and meditation that accompany each selection. Here the person is addressed in her/his entirety and wholeness. The material provided is directed to and intended to appeal to the intellect, the affective, the creative in a person. The exercises are skillfully developed to bring about the synthetic integration of the three. But this too is characteristic of the feminine, i.e., to bring together and make whole!

As a new generation of women and men become accustomed to imaging and speaking about God in feminine terms and categories, as such expression no longer seems strange, the church and its theology will have profited much. Our grasp of the holy, the divine, will be at a deeper, richer level. And certainly a vote of thanks will be due to authors like Bridget Mary Meehan who have initiated and helped to develop the conversation.

— Georgia Masters Keightley
Trinity College, Washington DC

Introduction

Using female imagery from the Bible, Christian tradition and contemporary women's experiences, this book of reflections builds on those proffered in *Exploring the Feminine Face of God*, inviting you to delight in additional in-depth experiences of God in feminine metaphor. Whether used in communal sharing or individual reflection, these meditations help to fill in the gaps in the Judeo-Christian tradition which regularly spoke of God throughout the ages in masculine language and imagery. If we do not mean that God is male when masculine imagery is used, perhaps we should ask ourselves if there should be a problem speaking of God in female imagery? I believe now is the time for both women and men not only to expand our images of God to include the feminine but to embrace and delight in the beauty, power, strength of the feminine in God and in ourselves. *Delighting in the Feminine Divine* offers liberating images for prayer and contemplation which women and men can use to enrich their spiritual lives.

It is my hope that individuals, groups and small intentional communities who use this book will find it a fruitful source of nourishment for prayer, reflection, discussion and faith-sharing. Using female images from the bible, tradition and women's experience, this book offers an approach for contemplating God firmly rooted in the female experience of the Christian tradition. Praying with feminine images of God introduces us into a wonderful variety of new possibilities for prayer that will enrich our spiritual growth and help us to transform political, social, economic, systems that oppress us. In her book *Called Into Her Presence*, Virginia Ann Froehle (Notre Dame: Ave Maria Press, 1992, pp. 19-20), invites us into a fantasy world which shows us dramatically how oppressive our diet of masculine images has been. She asks us to imagine what it would be like to grow up in a church like this:

> When people sing in church, they praise God's faithfulness, Her queenship and power over the universe, Her protective care. Sermons call everyone to be grateful to

Her, to trust in Her motherly love and to live by Her commands. Church windows and paintings present Her sometimes as a woman on a throne, sometimes as a lover reaching out Her arms, sometimes as the center and source of creation surrounded with the moon and stars, animals, trees, birds and human beings.

Leaders of the Eucharist are always women and every Mass is publicly offered for the salvation of all women or womankind. Men are included, of course, and are told so from the time they are small. After all, the words *woman* and *women* contain the words *man* and *men*. The lectors, address church readings to everyone as "My sisters in Christ," and ritual passages use many phrases like "women of God."

Some men and women want to change the feminine-only image of God or the use of *women* for both sexes or the calling forth of women only for priestly leadership. They are told that women more perfectly reflect the image of God as seen in the qualities of Jesus who was eminently noncompetitive, gentle, nurturing, understanding, nonviolent, and forgiving. The word *woman* is, therefore, more appropriate. It is God's will that women be Her chief ministers of the gospel.

Virginia Froehle urges us to ponder the effect that such a church would have on its members male and female, the environment, society, attitudes, prejudices and interactions between men and women. This dramatic contrast helps us see vividly the cultural effects of the past two thousand years of predominantly male imagery.

With *Delighting in the Feminine Divine* I hope to help you experience the mystery of God in a new and deeper way. Each of the four sections begins with introductory material, providing the reader with the theological and scriptural background for understanding the female metaphors presented in the reflections. After that you will find a quote from scripture, tradition, or contemporary women, nine prayer suggestions, and four discussion questions to enable you to explore the metaphor on your own. Contemplate each metaphor in a leisurely manner, experiencing the power of symbol in the illustrations to draw you into the mystery of the Feminine Divine. As you do so, be aware of the insights, feelings and images that emerge. You may wish to respond in journaling, poetry, or some artistic form such as drawing, sculpting, needlepoint, mandala, dance or the rhythmic bodily movement of mime. In the prayer suggestions, I describe a variety of approaches for reflection. You may use them in order or skip around, trying one that appeals to you. If you find one unappealing, move to another style until you find the one that attracts you. Today one suggestion may help you experience the Feminine Divine; while tomorrow another may launch your new insights of divine mystery. Do not force yourself to use material which you intuitively shy away from. Respect the messages of your own subconscious. You may wish to ask yourself, however, what life-experience makes you uncomfortable with this or that image.

Delighting in the Feminine Divine is also written for group use. Groups could use one or more of the discussion questions as a rich resource for delighting in God by mutual sharing. For prayer you might read aloud one reflection and one or more of the prayer suggestions and then listen together to what God is revealing. Background music may be helpful. Choose something quieting and instrumental rather than lyrical. Groups could then share their experiences and/ or their responses to the discussion questions with one another. Larger groups could break into small share-groups for the initial prayer and discussion, later rejoining for a corporate share-time. Group work may give birth to liberating ways of addressing the divine mystery in corporate prayer—a first step in expanding the public images of God in our communal worship. This would indeed be a major contribution to the spiritual life of the entire church.

Part One

The Feminine Divine in the Hebrew Scriptures

Even though the Hebrew tradition affirms God's transcendence of sexuality, it often refers to God in masculine, and occasionally in feminine images. The masculine images are well known: e.g. God as caring father, courageous warrior, strong king, jealous husband, ruling lord etc. Feminine images are less familiar: God as comforting mother, gentle midwife, a woman in labor, nursing mother, mother of humanity. Elizabeth Johnson, in her recent book *She Who Is* (New York: Crossroad, 1992) comments on some female metaphors for the Spirit, which appear in the Hebrew Scriptures: "Whether hovering like a nesting mother bird over the egg of primordial chaos in the beginning (Gn.1:2), or sheltering those in difficulty under the protective shadow of her wings (Ps. 17:8, 36:7, 57:1,61:4 91:1,4 Is. 31:5) or bearing the enslaved up on her wings toward freedom (Ex. 19:4 Dt. 32:11-12) divine Spirit activity is evoked with allusion to femaleness." (*She Who Is,* p. 83.)

In the Jewish tradition the Spirit of God was described by the feminine image of the *shekinah*. *Shekinah* is the feminine Hebrew word for "dwelling" and can be translated literally as "the one who dwells." *Shekinah* designates God's presence dwelling among the people, and is spoken of in a number of texts (Ex. 25:8; 29:45-46). It was first used to avoid referring to God directly, out of respect. Instead of saying that God's Spirit descended on the Holy of Holies, the rabbis say that the *shekinah* dwells here, meaning God's powerful feminine presence is among us. (*She Who Is* p. 85.)

The *shekinah* appears in the symbols of cloud, light and fire accompanying and giving hope to the Israelites as they journeyed through the darkness of wilderness and exile, so that "wherever the righteous go, the *shekinah* goes with them." (Genesis Rabbah 86.6, Dale Moody, "Shekinah" *Interpreters Dictionary of the Bible* (Nashville, Tenn.: Abingdon, 1962) 4:317-19) Heschel suggests that when the people suffer, the *shekinah* suffers with them. "When a human being suffers what does the Shekinah say? My head is too heavy for Me; My arm is too heavy for Me. And if God is so grieved over the blood of the wicked that is shed, how much more so over the blood of the righteous." (Abraham Heschel, *God in Search of Man*: A Philosophy of Judaism (New York: Harper & Row, 1955) 21-22 and 80-87. quoted in *She Who Is,* p. 86) Furthermore, the *shekinah* promises to be involved in the human struggle as "She-Who-Dwells-Within, divine compassionate love, source of strength for all those who need comfort." (*She Who Is* pp. 85-86.)

I HAVE LOOKED AWAY,
AND KEPT SILENCE,
I HAVE SAID NOTHING
HOLDING MYSELF IN;
BUT NOW, I CRY
OUT AS A WOMAN IN
LABOR, GASPING
AND PANTING.

IS. 42:14

Through the centuries most of this maternal imagery describing the Spirit's activity was attributed to Mary, mother of Jesus, as a mirror of the Divine, and to holy mother the church. "The symbol of the maternity of the Spirit was virtually forgotten, along with Spirit/Shekinah's capacity as a term to evoke divine presence and activity in female form. But this resonance abides in the texts of Scripture and tradition, offering one resource for emancipatory speech about God." (*She Who Is*, p. 86)

The Hebrew Scriptures contain other beautiful images reflecting the feminine qualities of the Divine. In Deuteronomy, in the song of Moses, God describes herself in the motherly reproach: "You were unmindful of the rock that bore you (*yladeka*) and you forgot the God who writhed in labor pains with you (*meholeleka*)." (Deut. 32:18) In Hebrew, the word *rehem* means womb. The plural form, *rahamim*, signifies mercy, compassion love. To speak of God's mercy or compassion in the Bible is to describe God's motherly-womb love. This motherly womb-love of God appears in the Scriptures in a number of places. The passage of Jer. 31:15-22 expresses Yahweh's motherly compassion for Ephraim (v 20): "Is Ephraim my dear Son? my darling child? For the more I speak of him, the more do I remember him. Therefore, my womb trembles for him; I will truly show motherly-compassion (*rachem arachamennu*) upon him." (Phyllis Trible, *God and the Rhetoric of Sexuality*, Fortress Press, 1978 p. 45.) The passage Jer. 31:15-22 emphasizes that the male was born from the female's womb: "For Yahweh has created a new thing in the land: female surrounds (*tesobeb*) man." (Jer. 31:22) As Phyllis Trible observes (*God and the Rhetoric of Sexuality* p. 50.) "The very form and content of the poem embodies a womb: woman encloses man. The female organ nourishes, sustains, and redeems the male child Ephraim."

Yahweh, through Second Isaiah, describes herself as screaming out in labor pains: "I have looked away, and kept silence, I have said nothing, holding myself in; But now, I cry out as a woman in labor, gasping and panting." (Is. 42:14-New American Bible); and as a tender mother with a child at the breast: "Can a mother forget her infant be without tenderness for the child of her womb? Even should she forget I will never forget you" (Is. 49:15-New American Bible). Comparing her concern for exiled Israel to that of a mother for her own infant, Yahweh cries out: "Listen to me, house of Jacob and all the remnant of the house of Israel who have been born by me from the belly (*beten*), carried from the womb (*racham*), even until old age I am the one, and to gray hairs am I carrying you. Since I have made, I will bear, carry and save.

3

(Is. 46:3-4, translation: Swidler, *Biblical Affirmations of Woman*, p. 33.). (Source: Swidler, *Biblical Affirmations of Woman*, pp. 31-33)

Contemporary biblical scholars are working diligently to bring to light little known imagery of the feminine Divine. D.F. Stramara translates *El Shaddai* (a name for the Divine in the Hebrew Scripture) as "God the breasted one." In Hebrew, the word for breast is *shad*, and *ai* is the feminine ending. Stramara hints that "one need only look at the shape of a mountain to grasp its origin." It is interesting to note that these scripture experts also point out that *El Shaddai* is used to refer to the breath or Spirit of God as in Job 33:4 "God's breath it was that made me, the breathing of *Shaddai* that gave me life." [D. F. Stramara, "El Shaddai: A Feminine Aspect of God" (Pecos, New Mexico: Dove Publications), pamphlet quoted in *Created in Her Image* p. 10.]

Tasks traditionally attributed to women appear as another source of feminine images portraying divine activity in human life. God is pictured as a woman knitting together new life in a mother's womb

(Ps. 139:13), as an elegant seamstress sewing clothing for the first couple in Genesis 3:21. In Ps. 22:9-10 God is described as a midwife bringing forth life from the womb. She is spoken of as a washerwoman "cleansing the bloodstains of Jerusalem," (Is. 4:4 New Revised Standard) washing away our sin and removing our guilt in Ps. 51:7-9). (*She Who Is,* p. 83.)

Delight in, contemplate, discuss and share your experiences of the Feminine Divine in the following passages from the Hebrew Scriptures.

A Hovering Nesting Mother Bird

Scripture

In the beginning, when God created the heavens and the earth, the earth was a formless void, and darkness covered the face of the deep, while a wind from God swept over the face of the waters. (Genesis 1:1-2, *NRSV*)

Questions for Personal Reflection or Group Discussion

1. What feelings, insights, images does the image of the Spirit giving birth to the world stir within you?

2. Think about the earth today. What challenges do we face in caring for the earth? How can we be good earth-keepers and stewards of creation?

3. How do you give birth to new life? How is the Spirit active in your efforts to develop a more reverent attitude toward all creatures? life? people?

4. What can you do to express your compassion toward earth's creatures.

Prayer Suggestions

1. Breathe slowly and deeply. As you are breathing be aware that God's maternal Spirit is breathing new life into you.

2. Read the story of creation in your bible in Genesis 1:1-31 slowly and imagine the Spirit of God as a mother bird nesting over the chaos, bringing forth light from darkness, sky and water, earth and plants, animals and human life, giving birth to the world.

3. The Hebrew word for Spirit (*Ruach*) is feminine in form. The writer of Genesis(1:2) tells that the Spirit "moved" (*rachaph*) or "fluttered over" the waters to bring forth creation. Deut. 32:11 uses this same word to describe God as a mother eagle "fluttering over" her young eaglets. As you reflect on the maternal Spirit "fluttering over" creation, what thoughts, images, feelings, sensations, memories, insights, are you aware of? Imagine the Spirit giving birth to the world . . . to you.

4. Does this image of the Spirit as a nesting mother bird giving birth to the world give you any new appreciation of your connectedness with and compassion for earth's creatures? If so,

describe this relationship. Select something of the earth and be-friend it (a rock, bird, tree, flower . . .) What does this gift of creation tell you about God? your life? the earth? You might wish to write a dialogue describing what this creation gift "says" to you.

5. Celebrate your connectedness with the earth by walking with the sun, moon, stars, plants and animals . . . Talk with them as friends and invite them to tell you the creation story. Open yourself to the surprises the nurturing Spirit has hidden within them. Thank them for all that they have revealed to you of divine mystery in creation. Share your dreams for the earth with them.

6. Use your senses to become one with creation. Be aware of how the air smells, the sounds you hear. Sit or lay down and feel the earth around you. Look at the sky, clouds, flowers, plants, trees, animals, sun, stars as if you were seeing them for the first time. Become one with the Spirit and contemplate Her beauty shining in the faces of all creation.

7. What thoughts, feelings, images, sensations, memories, insights, do you experience?

8. Become aware that the Spirit is birthing creation today. In what ways do you experience the Spirit giving birth to the world? What "new awarenesses" is the Spirit creating in our time? How can you become more involved in the Spirit's maternal activity?

9. Record your feelings, images, thoughts, insights, decisions in a journal, poetry, art, song, dance or in some other creative way.

Creating Human Life in Her Image

Scripture

Then God said: "Let us make humankind in our image, according to our likeness"; Genesis: 1:26 (*NRSV*)

Questions for Personal Reflection or Group Discussion

1. Yves Congar, in his book on the Holy Spirit, reflected: "There must be in God, in a transcendent form, something that corresponds to masculinity, and something that corresponds to femininity." Do you agree? If so why? If not why?

(Yves Congar *I Believe in the Holy Spirit,* vol. 3 (New York: Seabury Press, 1983, p. 155.)

2. If you are a woman do you see yourself as an image of God? How does this belief/experience affect your relationship with God? with others?

3. If you are a man do you see yourself as an image of God? How does this belief/experience affect your relationship with God? with others?

4. How can praying with feminine images of God help women and men reach greater wholeness by helping them to embrace their feminine side? How can praying with feminine images of God help you to reach greater wholeness by allowing you to embrace your feminine side?

Prayer Suggestions

1. Quiet your mind and body. Journey to the center point of your being.

2. Play some of your favorite music. Be aware that you are the image of God. Move or dance to the music to celebrate your identity.

3. As you reflect on yourself as a metaphor of God, be conscious of any thoughts, feelings, insights, memories, sensations that emerge. Record these, if you wish in a journal.

4. In what ways do you reflect God's feminine presence to others at the present time? Give thanks for these experiences.

5. Ask God to remove any obstacles that keep you from embracing your feminine side and sharing it with others. Share with God

any negative feelings you may have about your feminine side such as anger, hurt, disappointment, rage, hostility, fear . . .

6. Invite God to heal any hurt that you experienced in your relationship with your mother or any woman in your life that blocked you from experiencing God's feminine love. One approach to healing the feminine within us is to image God as the ideal Mother/Lover/Sister/Friend/Woman . . . Ask Her to embrace you with the unconditional love and affirmation you need to become a whole and holy image of Her Feminine Presence in the world.

7. A favorite prayer that I sometimes use is: "O Nurturing God, heal the difference between the love I needed and the love I received. Reach deep within me as I rest in your womb; you who loved me into existence; and soothe away any pain or fear from my past."

8. Imagine God embracing you with Her presence . . . loving you beyond your greatest imaginings . . . gifting you with the special gifts and blessings you need . . . freeing you from debilitating fears . . . liberating you from damaging compulsions . . . protecting you from danger . . . strengthening you with new vision . . . empowering you with courage . . . helping you to discover the beauty of the feminine within you. etc.

9. Record your feelings, images, thoughts, insights, decisions in a journal, poetry, art, song, dance or in some other creative way.

KEEP ME AS THE APPLE OF YOUR EYE;
HIDE ME IN THE SHADOW OF YOUR WINGS
FROM THE WICKED WHO USE
VIOLENCE AGAINST ME. Psalm 17:8-9

Sheltering Those in Difficulty Under the Shadow of Her Wings

Scripture

Keep me as the apple of your eye;
>   hide me in the shadow of your wings
from the wicked who use violence against me.
(Psalm 17:8-9, *NAB*)

Hear, O God, my cry;
>   listen to my prayer!
From the earth's end I call to you
>   as my heart grown faint.
You will set me high upon a rock; you
>   will give me rest,
for you are my refuge,
a tower of strength against the enemy.
Oh, that I might lodge in your tent forever,
take refuge in the shelter of your wings!
(Psalm 61:2-5 *NAB*)

Scripture

Be merciful to me, O God, be merciful to me,
>   for in you my soul takes refuge.
In the shadow of your wings I will take refuge,
>   until the destroying storms pass by. (Psalm 57:2 *NRSV*)

Scripture

You who live in the shelter of the
>   Most High,
who dwell in the shadow of the
>   Almighty,
Say to God, "My refuge and
>   my fortress,
my God in whom I trust"
With her pinions she will cover you
>   and under her wings you shall take refuge;
her faithfulness is a shield and a buckler.
(Paraphrase of Psalm 91:1,2,4 adapted from *NRSV*)

Questions for Personal Reflection or Group Discussion

1. Think about the world today. Where do you see crisis and violence? What understandings or new insights does this maternal image of God provide?

2. Recall times in your life when you experienced God's protection. Do you believe God protects you at this moment, wherever you are? What word, image or symbol best expresses your experience of God's loving protection in your life?

3. As you reflect on the image of the Spirit as Mother Bird sheltering you in danger under the shadow of Her wings, do you feel God's protective presence in any new way?

4. How are you being called to trust in God's loving care in your life now? What obstacles keep you from trusting in Her loving protection? What do you think you can do about them?

Prayer Suggestions

1. You may wish to begin this prayer experience by using a mantra, a breath prayer that uses seven syllables. Breathe in on the first three syllables and breathe out on the last three syllables. The fourth syllable is the syllable in-between where you change from breathing in to breathing out. Spend five or ten minutes reciting your prayer mantra as you focus on this feminine image of God. Choose one of the following mantras or create your own:

> "I take refuge in your love,"
> "Protect me, under your wings,"
> "Mother God, I trust in you."

2. Then use your imagination as you read the scripture above to image God as a protective mother bird guarding you from danger in the shelter of her wings. What new understandings of God do you experience as you reflect on this image? Does this new knowledge empower you? What images or feelings does it evoke?

3. Share with God the dangers/crises you now face. Listen as God responds to each of your concerns. God asks you to trust in Her protective care. What images or feelings come to mind when you think about this? Are they positive or negative images or feelings?

Share with God your response to Her invitation.

4. Ask God for the courage and strength you need in times of crisis or danger. Be aware of any changes (in life-style, job, environment, relationships etc.) that you may need to make in order to choose life, health, healing and wholeness in your life.

5. God, our protective Mother suffers with the poor, homeless, sick, starving, destitute people of the world who experience violence, war, famine, prejudice in their daily lives. Pray these psalms as prayers of intercession for their deliverance.

6. Imagine God weeping with the poor, needy and destitute of every land. God's heart breaks as She experiences the suffering of Her people, the evils of suffering, starvation, violent crime and death. She gathers the human family under the shelter of her wings and listens to their cries for deliverance, healing and empowerment.

7. Ask yourself this question, "What can I do to alleviate the sufferings of the poor and destitute in my family? neighborhood? city? world? What difference might I make?" Write down your response to this question and decide on one thing you can do to share God's love with others.

8. Reflect on the unjust structures that cause poverty, violence, famine, war. Has your experience of God's motherly love sheltering those in difficulty under the protective shadow of her wings given you a new vision for the welfare of the human family? What difference might it make? What images of a more just, peaceful global society might emerge?

9. Record your feelings, images, thoughts, insights, decisions in a journal, poetry, art, song, dance or in some other creative way.

Eagle/Spirit Winging the Enslaved Toward Freedom

Scripture

Thus shall you say to the house of Jacob, tell the Israelites. You have seen for yourselves how I treated the Egyptians and how I bore you up on eagle wings and brought you here to myself. Therefore, if you hearken to my voice and keep my covenant, you shall be my special possession, dearer to me than all other people though all the earth is mine. (Exodus 19 4-5 *NAB*)

Questions for Personal Reflection/Group Discussion

1. What insights did you discover about God as you explored this image of a female eagle bearing the enslaved up on wings toward freedom? How does it feel to image the God who liberated the Israelites from bondage this way?

2. Who are the enslaved in our contemporary society?

3. Who are the oppressors in our contemporary society?

4. What do you see as your ministry to the oppressed? to the oppressors? What do you need to do to accomplish this ministry?

Prayer Suggestions

1. Be aware of any tense areas in your body. Release the tension by tensing up a given muscle and then relaxing it. Do this with the major muscle areas throughout your body until you feel relaxed.

2. Do you remember a time when you felt oppressed by someone or something in your life?

3. How did you feel? What was it like for you? What was happening in you? in others? in the situation? What has this experience revealed to you about God? grace? sin? oppression? liberation?

4. Did you discover God's freeing love in any new way because of this experience? What did you learn about yourself from this experience? As you reflect on this experience what insights, feelings, thoughts, images, memories, sensations are you conscious of?

5. Imagine the Spirit of God as a powerful female eagle bearing you up on her wings carrying you to freedom. Allow yourself to

soar with Her to new heights. Open yourself to receive whatever you need to be set free and to become empowered with the courage, strength, peace . . . you need in your life right now. How does this experience make you feel? What do you think God is revealing to you about yourself? others? relationships? the oppressed and their oppressors?

6. What are the most important things you discovered about God as you explored this metaphor? What new images or understandings of God have you experienced through this reflection on God as female eagle carrying you to freedom?

7. Is there anything you feel you need to do as a result of this prayerful encounter with Eagle/Spirit God? Are there any changes you need to make in your life to become more free, liberated or empowered?

8. Think about ways you can share God's liberating, empowering love with the oppressed and their oppressors. Decide on one specific way you will do this.

9. Record your feelings, images, thoughts, insights, decisions in a journal, poetry, art, song, dance or in some other creative way.

Shekinah: She-Who-Dwells-Within

Scripture

They shall make a sanctuary for me, that I may dwell in their midst. (Exodus 25:8 *NAB*)

Questions for Personal Reflection or Group Discussion

1. *Shekinah* signifies God as *She-Who-Dwells-Within*, divine love in compassionate involvement with God's people. What image, symbol or word reflects the *Shekinah* in your life?

2. What new insights, understandings of God does *She-Who-Dwells-Within* reveal? How do you feel about it?

3. What can you to develop and nurture these insights?

4. How can praying in the presence of *She-Who-Dwells-Within* enrich your spiritual journey?

Prayer Suggestions

1. Spend a few minutes in silence. Concentrate on your breathing. As you breathe in, image *She-Who-Dwells-Within* you breathing in you, filling you with Her presence. As you breathe out, breathe out her presence to all creation.

2. As you reflect on this metaphor of God, be conscious of any thoughts, feelings, insights, memories, sensations that emerge. Record these, if you wish in a journal.

3. Close you eyes and image *She-Who-Dwells-Within* present in you. You are the sanctuary of *Shekinah*. What images come to mind when you experience yourself as *Shekinah's* dwelling place? Be conscious of any positive or negative feelings that occur. Share these with *Shekinah*.

4. Share your feelings about your self-identity with *Shekinah*. Be aware of any images that come to mind. How does this awareness of who you are as a person shape your spirituality?

5. Ask *Shekinah* for the gift of a deeper awareness of Her presence within you.

6. Spend at least five minutes now being completely still with *She-Who-Dwells-Within*. Simply be with *Shekinah* and delight in Her presence within you.

7. Now spend another five minutes in silence, be attentive to what *Shekinah* is revealing to you about your needs.

8. Open your hands as a sign of yielding yourself to *Shekinah*. Invite *Shekinah* to minister to these needs in whatever way She desires.

9. Record your feelings, images, thoughts, insights, decisions in a journal, poetry, art, song, dance or in some other creative way.

Shekinah: Transforming the Church

Scripture

I will dwell among the Israelites, and I will be their God. And they shall know that I am . . . their God, who brought them out of the land of Egypt that I might dwell among them; I am . . . their God." (Exodus 29:45-46 *NRSV*)

Questions for Personal Reflection or Group Discussion

1. *Shekinah* accompanies the people through the wilderness into the Promised Land. *She-Who-Dwells-Within* walks with the people of God over the rugged terrains and bleak deserts they encounter. How is the church a sign of *Shekinah-She-Who-Dwells-Within*? What evidence do you see of *Shekinah's* presence in the contemporary church?

2. When you look at the institutional church today, what ways, if any, does it appear to be challenged? How do you feel about these challenges?

3. How is *Shekinah* liberating, healing and transforming the church both as an institution and a community of disciples today?

4. In what ways is *Shekinah* calling us as a community of disciples to participate in the transformation of patriarchy in church and society?

Prayer Suggestions

1. Become still in the presence of *Shekinah*. You may wish to try a centering exercise such as listening to your heartbeat. *She-Who-Dwells-Within* is present in every heartbeat and breath you take.

2. When in silence you have become attentive to *Shekinah*, read Exodus 29:45-46.

3. Reflect on *Shekinah's* presence in the church through the centuries. Remember the times of the past when *Shekinah* helped the church proclaim the reign of God. Realize that there is no experience that the people of God have had that *Shekinah* is not present-no matter how difficult or painful. Think about how the church has been a sign of *Shekinah*. Give thanks to *Shekinah* for her presence in the church in ages past.

4. Now reflect on *Shekinah's* presence in the contemporary church.

Be aware of the ways *Shekinah* is working through the church to bring about the reign of God. Reflect on how the contemporary church is a sign of *She-Who-Dwells-Within*. Give thanks to *Shekinah* for Her presence with us today.

5. Invite *Shekinah* to heal the hurts that the people of God have experienced in their relationships with the institutional church.

Image *Shekinah* healing hurts caused by polarization between conservatives and liberals . . . Vatican officials and theologians . . . feminists and church officials etc. . . . Image her filling each person/group with new openness to each other . . . Imagine *She-Who-Dwells-Within* creating a church where the reign of God is lived fully . . . where justice and equality prevail . . . where patriarchal structures are transformed . . . where all members respect one another as the discipleship of equals . . . and where all are invited to use their gifts to serve the community.

6. As you reflect on *She-Who-Dwells-Within* transforming the church, be conscious of any images, thoughts, feelings, insights that emerge.

7. Make a list of several people who reflect *Shekinah's* presence in the church. Thank *Shekinah* for each one. Write a note to one of these persons describing how she/he is a reflection of God's feminine presence in the church.

8. Ask *Shekinah* how you can reflect Her presence to others and what you can do to participate in the transformation of patriarchal structures in church and society. Listen to what *She-Who-Dwells-Within* reveals to you.

9. Record your feelings, images, thoughts, insights, decisions in a journal, poetry, art, song, dance or in some other creative way.

El Shaddai: God the Breasted One

Scripture

"God's breath it was that made me, the breathing of *Shaddai* that gave me life."

Job 33:4 (Translation D.F. Stramara, "El Shaddai: A Feminine Aspect of God" (Pecos: New Mexico: Dove Publications) pamphlet quoted in Eleanor Rae & Bernice Marie-Daily, *Created In Her Image* New York: Crossroad, 1990 p. 10)

Questions for Personal Reflection or Group Discussion

1. D. F. Stramara translates *El Shaddai* (a name for the Divine in the Hebrew Scripture as "God the breasted one.") What new insights or understandings about God do you discover through this image?

2. What images of God come from your reflection on women's sexuality? How do you feel about these images?

3. What images, feelings, insights express your experience of your sexuality?

4. How does your sexuality affect your spirituality?

Prayer Suggestions

1. Breathe slowly, deeply and rhythmically in through your nose so that the abdomen rises on the in-breath and lowers as you breathe out through your mouth. As you do so, imagine *Shaddai* breathing new life into every area of your body. Spend several minutes doing this breathing exercise.

2. Become aware of the emotions you are feeling now. Feel them. What joys are you feeling? . . . What feelings of love and affection? . . . What feelings of peace? . . . What anxieties? . . . What feelings of sadness or loss? . . . What guilts? . . . What angers?

3. Give yourself as you are, with all your feelings to *Shaddai.*

4. Relax in *Shaddai's* passionate, boundless love for you. Allow that love to permeate ever fiber of your being.

5. Spend some time in quiet reflection sharing your feelings about your sexuality with *Shaddai.* How does your experience of

your sexuality affect your relationship with *Shaddai*? with others? with yourself?

6. Image yourself as a powerful, passionate reflection of *Shaddai*. Delight in your beauty and goodness. Give thanks to *Shaddai* for the gift of your sexuality.

7. As you reflect on yourself as an image of *Shaddai*, how do you feel? What new understanding of God do you experience? What new image of yourself do you experience?

8. Decide on one thing you will do to nurture a deeper awareness of your sexuality and spirituality.

9. Record your feelings, images, thoughts, insights, decisions in a journal, poetry, art, song, dance or in some other creative way.

Humanity in the Womb of God

Scripture

> Is Ephraim my dear Son? my darling child?
> even the more I speak of him,
> the more do I remember him.
> Therefore, my womb trembles for him;
> I will truly show motherly-compassion
> (*rachem arachamennu*) upon him.
> (Jeremiah 31:20, translation from Phyllis Trible, *God and the Rhetoric of Sexuality*, p. 45; Fortress Press, 1978)

Listen to me, house of Jacob and all the remnant of the house of Israel who have been borne by me from the belly (*beten*), carried from the womb (*racham*), even until old age I am the one, and to gray hairs am I carrying you. Since I have made, I will bear, carry and save. (Is. 46:3-4) (Translation Leonard Swidler, *Biblical Affirmations of Woman*, Philadelphia, Westminister Press, 1979, p. 33)

Questions for Personal Reflection or Group Discussion

1. What is your reaction to the image of humanity in the womb of God?

2. How can this image nurture and deepen your understanding of Mother God's compassionate love for all humanity? for all creation?

3. What vision does this image provide of our relationship with all creation?

4. If we embrace all creation as our sisters and brothers in the community of life, what difference might this make in how we approach ecological and environmental issues?

Prayer Suggestions

1. Relax your body and your mind. Become still and centered. Soft instrumental music may provide a beautiful background for this prayer experience.

2. Read these passages of Scripture. Image yourself in God's womb. What shapes, colors, sounds, textures do you experience? Let yourself be nurtured, cherished and loved. Allow God's com-

passionate tenderness to penetrate and fill your entire being. How does it feel to loved by God, your Mother? Be aware of any thoughts, feelings, sensations, or insights that emerge.

3. Give thanks to God for any new ways you experienced her motherly womb love. Ask God to help you be aware that you dwell always in the fullness of Her love.

4. Now image humankind and all creation in God's womb. All persons and creatures come from and image Mother God. All creation is interconnected women and men . . . birds and elephants . . . trout and turtles . . . bees and roses . . . All experience the trembling of God's womb and motherly compassion.

5. Imagine God forever giving birth to all creation. Experience yourself and all creation filled with life-giving power. Be aware of any thoughts, feelings sensations or insights that emerge.

6. Imagine the earth and all her creatures as a living organism. The moon, sun, planets, and stars are our sisters and brothers in the community of life. All of us are partners in being brought forth from God's womb with creative power to give life to one another.

7. Reflect on how the image of creation in God's womb and our experience of the earth as a living organism can bring new insights and understandings to address the current ecological crisis. Write down any insights or understandings that come to you.

8. Be aware of anything God is trying to reveal to us, to our world, to our nation, to our church through this environmental crisis. Ask God to show what you can do now to contribute to the ecological movement.

9. Record your feelings, images, thoughts, insights, decisions in a journal, poetry, art, song, dance or in some other creative way.

Washerwoman God

Scripture

Cleanse me of sin with hyssop, that I may be purified; wash me, and I shall be whiter than snow. (Psalm 51:9 *NAB*)

Questions for Personal Reflection or Group Discussion

1. Write in this space words, images, feelings, sensations that describe what it feels like to be washed clean, purified, cleansed by Washerwoman God.

2. As you reflect on your life at the present time, can you identify some area in you that needs cleansing, salvation, purification, forgiveness, redemption?

3. As you reflect on the world around you, can you give some examples of sinful structures or situations that keep people from experiencing liberation, freedom, human rights such as sexual/racial/age/ disability discrimination, genocide, ethnic cleansing, sexual exploitation, domination, war etc.

4. How can you collaborate with women of different races, classes, and ages to bring about peace, equality, justice and change in our world?

Prayer Suggestions

1. Take a shower or bath, or imagine yourself taking a shower or bath. Feel the water flowing and splashing all over you, cleansing, refreshing and relaxing your entire body.

2. As you bathe, invite God the washerwoman to reveal to you any attitude(s) or habit(s) of sin that need(s) Her redeeming love.

3. Share with Washerwoman God any guilt, regret, or shame you have about these sinful areas of your life. Express your desire to change and repent. Invite Washerwoman God to cleanse your sin, wash away your guilt with the saving waters of Her divine forgiveness, and refresh you with joy and peace.

4. Thank Washerwoman God for making you whiter than snow and for strengthening you in the areas of weakness you have identified.

5. Pray for the grace to be a reflection of Washerwoman's God saving, empowering love in your relationships.

6. Ask Washerwoman God to redeem the world of social sin by removing sinful structures and attitudes that oppress God's people.

7. Imagine Washerwoman God cleansing the world of its sin and destructive evil. See Her scrubbing away the filth of discrimination, prejudice, hatred, violence, war, domination, exploitation etc.

8. Ask Washerwoman God to reveal to you how you can collaborate with woman of different races, classes, and ages to bring about peace, equality, justice and change in our world.

9. Record your feelings, images, thoughts, insights, decisions in a journal, poetry, art, song, dance or in some other creative way.

God as Seamstress

Scripture

Truly you have formed my inmost being; you knit me in my mother's womb. (Psalm 139:13 *NAB*)

And Yahweh God made tunics of skins for the man and his wife and clothed them. (Genesis 3:21) (translation in Swidler's *Biblical Affirmations of Woman*, p. 30)

Questions for Personal Reflection or Group Discussion

1. Reflect on the image of God as a Seamstress. Does this image reflect any new understandings or insights into divine providence?

2. How have you experienced the divine Seamstress' care in your life?

3. In what ways do you see the divine Seamstress at work in the world?

4. What can do to show the Seamstress' care for the world?

Prayer Suggestions

1. Begin your prayer by focusing on a favorite piece of clothing, quilt, tablecloth, afghan, needlepoint, tapestry etc. Remember how it was sewn, knit, crocheted together. Give thanks for its beauty and for the person who created it. Spend a few minutes simply being with this creative work in quiet appreciation.

2. Pray Psalm 139:13 over and over again. As you pray this psalm, image God, the divine Seamstress knitting you together in your mother's womb. Be conscious of Her provident care as she creates you in all your uniqueness and specialness. You are like no other person the Seamstress has made.

3. Reflect on a past experience you have had of God's provident care in your life. Be aware of any thoughts, feelings, insights or images that emerge from your reflection on this experience.

4. Imagine your life as a beautiful tapestry that God the Seamstress and you are working on together. Observe the Seamstress sewing, cutting, tieing and weaving different threads that you give her. Threads of bright and dark colors seem to blend together reflecting your joys and sorrows, highs and lows, strengths and weaknesses. Spend some time contemplating your life as a mag-

nificent tapestry! You may wish to create a tapestry of your life by using yarn, thread, material etc. As you do so, be aware of any images, symbols, feelings, insights or understandings that emerge.

5. Share with the Seamstress your appreciation for all She has done for you and any questions or insights that you have about your tapestry. Listen to the Seamstress' response to you.

6. Imagine the world as a tapestry that God the Seamstress is weaving. Observe the Seamstress working with the people of the world on the grand divine design—peace and justice. See Her cutting, sewing, tieing, knotting, weaving, the threads of love, truth, courage, compassion, kindness, together with the threads of pain, suffering, fear, guilt, etc. into a magnificent tapestry.

7. Share with the Seamstress your appreciation for all She has done for the world community and any questions or insights that you have about Her grand design for the world. Listen to the Seamstress' response to you.

8. Ask the Seamstress what you can do to participate in Her grand divine design for the world.

9. Record your feelings, images, thoughts, insights, decisions in a journal, poetry, art, song, dance or in some other creative way.

Part Two

The Feminine Divine
in
Sophia and Jesus-Sophia

In the Hebrew, Greek, and Latin languages, wisdom is of feminine grammatical gender *hokmah* in Hebrew, *sophia* in Greek, *sapientia* in Latin. Wisdom is the feminine aspect of the one God and is personified as a woman in the Bible. *Sophia* is the Greek word for wisdom, or more accurately a transliteration of that word. Using the name "*Sophia*" rather than "wisdom," which suggests a person rather than a concept, is the intention of the biblical writers. (Source: Susan Cady, Marian Ronan, Hal Taussig: *Wisdom's Feast*, San Francisco: Harper & Row, 1989, p. 16.) Elizabeth Johnson, scholar and author points out that the Bible consistently describes Wisdom as female, portraying her as mother, sister, female lover, hostess, preacher, and a variety of other female roles "wherein she symbolizes transcendent power ordering and delighting in the world. She pervades the world, both nature and human beings, interacting with them all to lure them along the right path to life." (*She Who Is,* New York: Crossroad, 1991, p. 87)

What images of *Sophia*, Holy Wisdom, do we discover in the Bible? *Sophia* is a woman of strength and knowledge who is part of the ongoing creative process of the world and is the source of all good things: "She deploys her strength from one end of the earth to the other, ordering all things for good . . . Her closeness to God lends luster to her noble birth, since the Lord of all has loved her. Yes, she is an initiate in the mysteries of God's knowledge. She makes choice of the works God is to do" (Wisdom 8:1, 3-4).

Sophia is a woman of wisdom. In Proverbs 4:1,2,5,6, the biblical writer comments: "Listen my children, to a father's instruction; pay attention, and learn what clear perception is. What I am commending to you is sound doctrine: do not discard my teaching. Acquire *Sophia*, acquire perception; Never forget her, never deviate from my words, Do not desert her, she will keep you safe, love her, she will watch over you." In Wisdom 6, *Sophia* is pictured as the process of knowing or learning. In verse 13, it is said of her: "Quick to anticipate those who desire her, she makes herself known to them." This "making known" is described in verse 17 as the process of learning or acquiring wisdom: "Of her the most sure beginning is the desire for discipline, care for discipline means loving her." Encountering *Sophia* requires concentration and study. A disciplined quest for wisdom and understanding leads to *Sophia*, the one who is at the heart of all knowledge and wisdom: "By those who love her she is readily seen, and found by those who look for her . . . in every thought of theirs, she comes to meet them" (Wisdom 6:12, 16).

Sophia is a liberator: "For she is more beautiful than the sun and excels every constellation of the stars. Compared with the light, she is found to be superior. For it is succeeded by the night, but against wisdom evil does not prevail" (Wisdom 7:29-30, *NRSV*). *Sophia* is likewise an advocate of transformation: "For within Sophia is a spirit intelligent, holy, unique, manifold, subtle, active, incisive, unsullied, lucid, invulnerable, benevolent, sharp, irresistible, beneficent, loving to women and men" (Wisdom 7:22).

Sophia is a woman of peace and discernment and a powerful teacher: "She fills their whole house with their heart's desire and their storerooms with her produce . . . The crown of [*Sophia*] makes peace and health flourish . . . the Lord has showered down learning and discernment with her and exalted the renown of those who hold her close" (Ecclesiasticus 1:17-20). Proverbs 8:1-11 portrays *Sophia* as impatient with the children of humanity whom she tries to instruct: "Does *Sophia* not call meanwhile? Does Discernment not lift up her voice? . . . she cries aloud, 'O people: I am calling you; my cry goes out to the children of humanity. You ignorant ones, study discretion; and you fools, come to your senses. Listen, I have serious things to tell you, and from my lips come honest words, My mouth proclaims the truth . . . All the words I say are right, nothing twisted in them, nothing false, all straightforward to the one who understands, honest to those who know what knowledge means. Accept my discipline rather than silver, knowledge in preference to gold. For wisdom is more precious than pearls, and nothing else is so worthy of desire.'" The one who learns from Sophia is rewarded with life and prosperity: "Acquire *Sophia,* acquire perception . . . Hold her close, and she will make you great; embrace her, and she will be your pride" (Proverbs 4:5,8).

Sophia is a woman of justice: "I love those who love me . . . I walk in the way of virtue in the paths of justice, enriching those who love me, filling their treasuries" (Proverbs 8:17, 20-21). "With me are riches and honor, lasting wealth and justice" (Proverbs 8:18).

Sophia is the lover of the Lord of all: "I fell in love with her beauty (says the sage), Her closeness to God lends luster to her noble birth, since the Lord of all loved her" (Wisdom 8:2-3). In Ecclesiasticus 6:26-28 Ben Sirach advises his followers: "Court her with all your soul, and with all your might keep her ways; go after her and seek her; she will reveal herself to you; once you hold her, do not let her go. For in the end you will find rest in her and she will take the form of joy for you." Another text which portrays *Sophia* as lover is found in Wisdom 8:9,16: "I therefore determined to take her to share my life, knowing she would be my counselor in prosperity, my comfort in cares and sorrow . . . When I go home I shall take my ease with her, for nothing is bitter in her company, when life is shared with her there is no pain, gladness only, and joy."

Sophia is the creator of the universe: "When God set the heavens in place, I was present, when God drew a ring on the surface of the deep, when God fixed the clouds above, when God fixed fast the wells of the deep, when God assigned the sea its limits—and the waters will not invade the land—when God established the foundations of the earth, I was by God's side, a master craftswoman, delighting God day after day, ever at play by God's side, at play everywhere in God's domain, delighting to be with the children of humanity" (Proverbs 8:27-31). *Sophia's* role in the creation of the world is also described in Ecclesiasticus: "I came forth from the mouth of the Most High and I covered the earth like a mist. I had my tent in the heights and my throne in a pillar of cloud, Alone I encircled the vault of the sky, and I walked on the bottom of the deeps" (Ecclesiasticus 24:3-5).

Sophia is mother.: "*Sophia* brings up her children and cares for those who seek her. Whoever loves her loves life, those who wait on her early will be filled with happiness . . . Whoever obeys her, judges aright and whoever pays attention to her dwells secure" (Ecclesiasticus 4:11-12,15). "Therefore I prayed and understanding was given to me; I called on God and the spirit of *Sophia* came to me. I preferred her to scepters and thrones, and I accounted wealth as nothing in comparison to Her . . . All good things came to me along with Her, and in Her hands accounted wealth, I rejoiced in them all, because Sophia leads them; but I did know that She was their mother. (Wisdom 7:7-8,32 *NRSV*)

Sophia, is an angry preacher crying aloud in the street, in the markets she raises her voice . . . "Sophia calls aloud in the streets, she raises her voice in the public squares; she calls out at the street corners. She delivers her message at the city gates, 'You ignorant people, how much longer will you cling to your ignorance? How much longer will mockers revel in their mocking and fools hold knowledge contemptible? Pay attention to my warning: now will I pour out my heart to you and tell you what I have to say'." (Proverbs 8:4-11)

There is more written about *Sophia* in the Hebrew scriptures than about Adam, Noah, Abraham, Sarah, or Miriam. Only God, Job, Moses, and David receive more attention in the scriptures. Commenting on the impact of *Sophia* in the Bible, Hal Taussig, Marian Ronan and Susan Cady make this observation: She is the "divine saving figure in history, guiding Noah to safety, calling Abraham, and leading Moses and the Hebrew people to safety through the sea. In fact, *Sophia* and God seem to be fully interchangeable, since halfway through the account of salvation history a male God replaces *Sophia* as the divine actor." (*Wisdom's Feast,* pp. 13-14)

Sophia is a significant symbol for contemporary women because she portrays the assertive, dynamic, activist woman. In the scriptures *Sophia* appears as an angry preacher who awakens us to the anger of God and helps us to express our anger with patriarchy in church and society. *Sophia*, Woman of Justice, challenges us to work in solidarity with the poor and oppressed for the transformation of unjust structures. *Sophia*, the Liberator, who sets free the oppressed and the oppressors, whether they are individuals or institutions, empowers us to participate in her saving action in our local communities. *Sophia*, Compassionate Woman, feels the pain, violence and abuse that women experience throughout the world. As Birther of Creation, *Sophia* reveals our connectedness with one another and all earth's creatures. *Sophia*, the Caring Mother, nurtures us and shows us how to nurture ourselves and others. Now more than ever we need to saturate our consciousness with Her imagery and presence. (Source: Unless otherwise indicated, the biblical translation and the research on *Sophia* contained in this chapter are found in *Wisdom's Feast,* pp. 13-27)

Jesus-Sophia

Who and where is *Sophia* in the Christian scriptures? According to a number of New Testament texts, Jesus is *Sophia*. Felix Christ in his scholarly work entitled *Jesus Sophia: Die Sophia Christologie bei den Synoptikern (Jesus Sophia: The Sophia Christology in the Synopitcs*—cited in *Wisdom's Feast,* p. 41) introduces Jesus as *Sophia* in Matthew, Mark, and Luke. In his book, Christ points out that the synoptics show Jesus speaking words similar to those of *Sophia*:

For example, in Matthew 11:28-30, Jesus says,

"Come to me, all you who labor and weary, and are carrying heavy burdens, and I will give you rest. Take my

32

yoke upon you, and learn from me; for I am gentle and humble in heart, and you will find rest for your souls. For my yoke is easy, and my burden is light." (Matthew 11:28-30, *NRSV*)

This resembles two passages in Sirach: "put your neck under her yoke and let your souls receive instruction; it is to be found close by. (Sirach 51:26, *NRSV*) and "Bend your shoulders and carry her, and do not fret under her bonds. Come to her with your soul, and keep her ways with all your might." (Sirach 6:25-26, *NRSV*)

In the Gospels of Matthew and Luke there are significant passages in which Jesus speaks words like that of *Sophia*. In Matthew 11:25-27 Jesus says:

"I bless you, Father, Lord of heaven and earth, for hiding these things from the learned and the clever and revealing them to mere children. Yes, Father, for that is what it pleased you to do. Everything has been entrusted to me by my Father, just as no one knows the Father except the Son and those to whom the Son chooses to reveal him." (Translation, *Wisdom's Feast*, p. 41.)

This text corresponds to the description of *Sophia* in the book of Wisdom 9:17-18:

"As for your [God's] intention, who could have learned it, had you not granted Sophia and sent your holy spirit from above? So have the paths of those on earth been straightened and people have been taught what pleases you, and have been saved by Sophia."

(Translation, *Wisdom's Feast*, p. 42)

Felix Christ also demonstrates how certain sayings of Jesus in Matthew and Luke presume a certain familiarity with *Sophia*. Some of these texts are: Matthew 11:16-19 Luke 7:31-35, Luke 10:21f, Matthew 23:34-36 Luke 11:49-51 Matthew 23:37-39 Luke 13:34f. In addition to this, Christ shows how Matthew, Mark and Luke's gospels describe Jesus as the bearer of wisdom. (Source: Cady, *Wisdom's Feast*, p. 41-42.)

Paul speaks of Jesus as the Christ, and then identifies Christ with Sophia: "We are preaching a crucified Christ who is the wisdom of (*Sophia*) of God" (1 Cor. 1:24-25). In the deutero-Pauline epistle to the Colossians there is a early church hymn (Col. 1:15-

20) which describes Jesus as the reflection of *Sophia* and as the one in whom the new creation unfolds:

> "He is the image of the invisible God, the first born of all creation; for in him all things in heaven and on earth were created, things visible and invisible, whether thrones or dominions or rulers or powers—all things have been created through him and for him. He himself is before all things and in him all things hold together." (Col. 1:15-17, *NRSV*)

(Source: Swidler, *Biblical Affirmations of Woman*, p. 62.)

In John's Gospel Jesus identifies himself (Jn. 6:35) in ways that reflect *Sophia*. Jesus, like *Sophia*, desires all people to come and eat and drink from him:

Jesus said to them, "I am the bread of life. Whoever come to me will never be hungry, and whoever believes in me will never be thirst." (Jn. 6:35, *NRSV*)

Sophia the Welcoming Hostess invites all to Her banquet:

"Come, eat of my bread and drink of the wine I have mixed. (Proverbs 9:5, *NRSV*)

This is similar, according to Leonard Swidler, "to the Prologue of John's Gospel where the Word, *Logos*, like *Hokmah-Sophia*, was said to be from the beginning with God, indeed, was God through whom all things were created, enlightening all humanity." (Swidler, p. 63) The description of Jesus as Word or *Logos* in John is similar to the description of *Sophia* in the Hebrew scriptures. What the author of the Prologue does is change *Sophia's* name to *Logos*, Word of God, and then identify this pre-existent, co-creator with Jesus. According to the eminent scholar Rudolf Bultmann the prologue of John was originally a *Sophia* hymn and *Logos* was substituted by the author of the Prologue. In summary, according to John, Jesus is *Sophia*. (Swidler, *Biblical Affirmations of Woman*, p. 63.)

Contemporary feminist theologians such as Elizabeth Johnson and Sandra Schneiders advocate using women's experiences and feminine imagery to describe the Christian experience of God. A new language, and new metaphors are needed in our church and world. Johnson seeks a liberating language to address the mystery of *Jesus-Sophia* in our midst that encompasses:

> "telling the gospel story of Jesus as the story of Wisdom's child, *Sophia* incarnate; by interpreting the sym-

bol of the Christ to allow its ancient inclusivity to shine through; by explicating christological doctrine to unlock what is of benefit." (*She Who Is,* p. 154) "The fundamental nature of Christian identity as life in Christ makes clear that the biblical symbol of Christ, the one anointed in the Spirit, cannot be restricted to the historical person Jesus nor to certain select members of the community"; Elizabeth Johnson claims, rather it "signifies all those who by drinking of the Spirit participate in the community of disciples . . . the body of the risen Christ becomes the body of the community; all are one Christ Jesus (1 Cor 12; Gal 3:28)."

She Who Is, p. 162.)

Sandra Schneiders agrees:

"the Christ is not exclusively the glorified Jesus, but the glorified Jesus animating his body which is the Church. Christ said to Paul "Why do you persecute me?" (Acts 9:4) because the literal fact is that the Christ is composed of all the baptized. This means that Christ, in contrast to Jesus, is not male, or more exactly not exclusively male. Christ is accurately portrayed as black, old, Gentile, female, Asian or Polish. Christ is inclusively all the baptized." (Schneiders, *Women and the Word* [see chap. 2, n. 57] p. 54.

In these reflections you are invited to pray with some new feminine images of God. Reflect on *Sophia's* different images—an angry preacher, liberator, mentor, hostess, mother. Meet *Jesus-Sophia* in the Christian scriptures. Allow the *Sophia* of the Hebrew scriptures to surprise you with creative ways of living and working together, new role models and alternatives to patriarchal stereotypes. Open yourself to *Sophia* incarnate in the Christian scriptures. Develop a relationship with *Jesus-Sophia*. Encounter *Sophia* for the first time, perhaps, in the Jesus stories of the Gospel. Observe how her feminine character changes the story. Be conscious that in *Jesus-Sophia* women's identity and sexuality are affirmed and identified with God. Dare to make one of the fundamental paradigm shifts of our time by delighting in the Feminine Divine!

Sophia: Angry Preacher

Scripture

Sophia calls aloud in the streets,
she raises her voice in the public squares;
she calls out at the street corners,
She delivers her message at the city gates,
"You ignorant people, how much longer will you cling to
your ignorance?
How much longer will mockers revel in their mocking
and fools hold knowledge contemptible?
Pay attention to my warning:
now will I pour out my heart to you,
and tell you what I have to say." (Proverbs 1:20-22)
"O people: I am calling you;
my cry goes out to the children of humanity.
You ignorant ones, study discretion;
and you fools come to your senses.
Listen I have serious things to tell you,
and from my lips come honest words.

My mouth proclaims the truth . . .
All the words I say are right,
nothing twisted in them, nothing false,
all straightforward to the one who understands,
honest to those who know what knowledge means.
Accept my discipline rather than silver,
knowledge in preference to gold.
For wisdom is more precious than pearls,
and nothing else is so worthy of desire."

(Proverbs: 8:4-11 translation by Susan Cady, Marian Ronan,
Hal Taussig, *Wisdom's Feast* San Francisco: Harper & Row, 1989,
pp. 20-21)

Questions for Personal Reflection or Group Discussion

1. Have you ever acted like an angry *Sophia*? How did you feel?
How did people respond to you? Are you being called to act like an
angry *Sophia* now?

2. In these texts, *Sophia* cries out, confronts, proclaims a de-
manding message that challenges Her listeners. Are you comfortable with this image of an angry *Sophia*? Can you name any

women today who remind you of an angry *Sophia*? How do you feel about them?

3. Beverly Harrison observes that "Anger is a mode of connectedness to others and it is always a vivid form of caring." Do you agree? Why? Why not? (Beverly Harrison, "The Power of Anger in the Work of Love," *Union Seminary Quarterly Review* 36 (1980-81, supplement) 49.

4. How can reflecting on *Sophia's* anger enable women to express their anger as a creative force for working against injustice? If you were asked to deliver a sermon on human rights, justice and equality for women today, what would you say?

Prayer Suggestions

1. Close your eyes. Relax your body. Focus on your breathing. Breathe slowly and deeply. As you breathe, imagine yourself in the presence of *Sophia,* the angry preacher.

2. Read this scripture passage in a loud voice as if you are *Sophia*—shouting in the streets . . . angry, impatient, furious, full of wrath. . . . Her message confronts and challenges . . . people walk away . . . *Sophia* threatens those who do not listen . . . *Sophia* complains that people reject Her . . . Allow yourself to feel *Sophia's* anger blazing up inside of you . . . Then, share with *Sophia* how it feels to be filled with Her righteous anger . . .

3. Ask *Sophia* to help you get in touch with and express *your* anger. Draw or write down, or make a list of your angry feelings and the causes or sources of your anger. Express your anger by screaming, pounding a pillow, punching a bag, running, dancing, rapping, jumping up and down, crying etc. As you do so, be aware that *Sophia* also is angry when you experience harm, violation, injustice, evil, abuse etc.

4. Ask *Sophia* to open you to Her love and healing power in the midst of your anger. Become aware of your inner strength and courage and decide how you can use your anger as an energizing force for change in your life and in the lives of those you love.

5. Invite *Sophia* to preach a sermon on transforming patriarchal structures in the church and society.

6. Listen to *Sophia* as She reproaches the church and society for its resistance to change, for legitimating political, social, economic structures that reinforce the domination and subordination of women.

7. Share with *Sophia* any feelings of anger and frustration you have experienced in working for justice and equality in the church and/or society.

8. Ask *Sophia* to use your anger as "a vivid form of caring," to bring about change in the church and society.

9. Record your feelings, images, thoughts, insights, decisions in a journal, poetry, art, song, dance or in some other creative way.

Sophia: Liberator

Scripture

> For she is more beautiful than the sun
> and excels every constellation of the stars.
> Compared with the light, she is found to be superior.
> For it is succeeded by the night,
> but against wisdom evil does not prevail.
> (Wisdom 7:29-30, *NRSV*)

Questions for Personal Reflection or Group Discussion

1. *Sophia's* saving power is among us and will ultimately triumph over all negativity, evil and sin. How have you experienced *Sophia's* saving power in your life?

2. Are there areas of your life where you need *Sophia's* saving power in the present?

3. As you look at the world around you, can you give some examples of *Sophia's* saving power at work?

4. In what ways can you share in *Sophia's* liberating work?

Prayer Suggestions

1. Slowly take a few breaths. Be aware of the air flowing through your nostrils as you breathe in and out. Allow your body to relax.

2. Open yourself to *Sophia's* saving presence as you read this passage. Be aware that *Sophia* will triumph over sin, evil and all that oppresses us.

3. Select an image, metaphor, word, or symbol from the text that touches you on a spiritual level.

4. Ponder its meaning. Dialogue with it. Contemplate its richness.

Allow it to fill you.

5. Allow a picture to form in your imagination that expresses the depth of *Sophia's* saving power in your life. Draw or paint a mandala (a sacred circle with a centerpoint that reflects the dialogue between the visible and invisible, the conscious and the unconscious). A mandala has two basic parts. The boundary which can be made from a variety of shapes to represent some symbolic

object or picture. The space within the boundary is divided up. It might look like a flower, rays of the sun, petals of a flower etc.) The centerpoint represents God's presence within us. A mandala is a visual centering form of prayer. You may wish to play beautiful music in the background as you paint or draw your mandala.

6. As you look at the mandala, breathe in the liberating love of *Sophia* that radiates from the mandala. Let it fill you with a deeper sense of *Sophia's* saving power in your life.

7. Breathe out the liberating love of *Sophia* that radiates from the mandala to all those who are suffering any form of sin, evil or oppression of in their lives.

8. During difficult times imagine yourself (another person/ group/ experiencing sin, evil, oppression) at the center of the mandala surrounded by *Sophia's* saving power. Allow the liberating love of *Sophia* radiating from your mandala to saturate and flow through you—freeing, healing, and empowering you throughout the day.

9. Record your feelings, images, thoughts, insights, decisions in a journal, poetry, art, song, dance or in some other creative way.

LIKE
A CEDAR
OF
LEBANON
I AM
RAISED
ALOFT...

Sophia: Tree of Life and Mentor

Scripture

Hold fast to instruction, never let her go;
keep her, for she is your life.   (Proverbs 4:13 *NAB*)

Like a cedar on Lebanon I am raised aloft,
like a cypress on Mount Hermon,
Like a palm tree in Engedi,
like a rosebush in Jericho,
Like a fair olive tree in the field,
like a plane tree growing beside the water.
Like a cinnamon or fragrant balm, or precious myrrh,
I give forth perfume;
Like galbanum and onycha and sweet spices,
like the odor of incense in the holy place.
I spread out my branches like a terebinth,
my branches so bright and so graceful.
I bud forth delights like the vine,
my blossom become fruit fair and rich.
Come to me, all you that yearn for me, and be filled
with my fruits;
You will remember me as sweeter than honey,
better to have than the honeycomb.
(Sirach 24:13-19 *NAB*)

Questions for Personal Reflection or Group Discussion

1. What does the image of *Sophia* as a tree or a beautiful plant reveal to you about the divine mystery?

2. In what ways have you connected or bonded with mentors who fostered your spiritual growth in the past?

3. Are you connecting or bonding with women and/or men who share similar issues or concerns now?

4. In what ways have you connected or bonded with *Sophia*?

Prayer Suggestions

1. Take some time to relax your body before you begin this reflection. Be aware of places in your body where you feel stress or tension. Breathe relaxation into each of these areas . . . head, neck, shoulders, arms, hands, fingers, chest, stomach, pelvis, hips,

thighs, knees, legs, ankles, toes. Be still and rest in Sophia's love for you.

2. Contemplate the beauty of a tree/plant. Touch, smell look, taste the fruit of the tree/plant. Invite the tree/plant to speak to you. Listen to what the tree/plant reveals to you about its connectedness to earth, creatures, sky, sun, stars, you . . . etc. Celebrate your connectedness with this tree/plant in a special way.

3. As you read the scripture passages from Proverbs and Sirach, imagine *Sophia* as a tree/plant. Be aware of what *Sophia* reveals to you about her connectedness with the earth, creatures, sky, sun, stars, you . . . etc.

4. Become aware of the ways you have experienced connectedness or bondedness with mentors who fostered your spiritual growth in the past. (parents, teachers, spiritual directors, role models etc.) Offer thanks for what you received in these relationships.

5. Recall relations now in which you experience bonding/connecting with other women or men who share similar issues or concerns. Be aware of any images, feelings, insights that occur as you reflect on these relationships. Name, affirm and offer thanks to *Sophia* for each gift given and received in some special way.

6. Reflect on any new experiences of bonding that may be occurring in your relationship with *Sophia*. Be aware of any images, feelings, insights that occur as you reflect on your relationship with Her. Name, affirm and give thanks for each gift given and received in some special way.

7. Celebrate your experience of connectedness/bonding with *Sophia* in some special way.

8. Cultivate this new relationship you have with *Sophia* by sharing Her with others. One way of doing this is by starting a *Sophia* group where women gather together to reflect on *Sophia's* presence, role and power in their lives and experiences as women.

9. Record your feelings, images, thoughts, insights, decisions in a journal, poetry, art, song, dance or in some other creative way.

Sophia: Welcoming Hostess

Scripture

> Sophia has built her house,
>> she has hewn her seven
>> pillars.
> She has slaughtered her animals,
>> she has mixed her wine,
>> she has also set the table.
> She has sent out her servant-girls, she calls
>> from the highest places in the town,
> "You that are simple, turn in
>> here!"
> To those without sense she says,
> "Come, eat of my bread and drink of the wine I have mixed.
> Lay aside immaturity, and live,
>> and walk in the way of
> insight."

(Proverbs 9:1-6 *NRSV*; I substituted *Sophia* for Wisdom)

Questions for Personal Reflection or Group Discussion

1. Does this scripture passage suggest any new images or names of God to you? What are they? Are you comfortable with them?

2. How did you feel as you watched *Sophia* prepare for the banquet described in this text?

3. Do you believe that *Sophia* invites you to Her table? Do you believe that *Sophia* invites all people to Her table?

4. How can you share *Sophia's* welcoming love by developing nurturing and supporting relationships in your life?

Prayer Suggestions

1. Close your eyes and relax in a quiet place. Become conscious of the pace and rhythm of your breathing. With each breath, let go of any concerns. Allow yourself simply "to be" in *Sophia's* presence.

2. As you read this Scripture passage, imagine *Sophia* as the builder, constructing her house . . . the butcher, slaughtering the animal(s) . . ., the vintner, mixing the wine . . . , the hostess,

sending her servants to announce the invitation . . . Picture yourself, your family, friends, neighbors, people of different races, nations, cultures etc. . . . sitting at the banquet table . . . enjoying the food and one another's company . . . Observe *Sophia* serving each guest . . . Look into *Sophia's* eyes as She serves you . . . Open yourself to Her gracious hospitality . . . Allow her nurturing love to fill you . . . Picture Her supportive love flowing through you in your loving service of others . . . Share your feelings with Her and the other guests . . .

3. Listen to *Sophia's* call to "lay aside immaturity and walk in the way of insight." Imagine the banquet participants talking excitedly about their efforts to live according to Her wisdom. Observe the tears and smiles as each one shares his/her journey. Share with *Sophia* and her guests the successes and failures you have experienced in living Her call.

4. Imagine yourself as a reflection of *Sophia*, the welcoming hostess. Picture yourself inviting people who are poor or who have special needs (single parents, families, elderly neighbors, unemployed friends, children, etc.) to a festive celebration in your home. How do you feel about each guest? How do they feel about you? What do you talk about? Record, if you wish, this conversation in your journal.

5. Reflect on ways you can nurture *Sophia's* love in your relationships. Make a list of these possibilities. Thank *Sophia* for these opportunities.

6. Decide on one thing you will do to nurture *Sophia's* love in your relationships with others.

7. Thank *Sophia* for the ways you have been nurtured and supported by others in your life.

8. Pray for all those who do not experience nurturing love in their relationships. Ask *Sophia* to fill them with Her nurturing, welcoming love.

9. Record your feelings, images, thoughts, insights, decisions in a journal, poetry, art, song, dance or in some other creative way.

SHE WILL
COME TO MEET THEM
LIKE A
MOTHER,...

SHE WILL
FEED THEM WITH THE
BREAD OF LEARNING,
AND GIVE THEM THE
WATER OF
WISDOM TO
DRINK. PARAPHRASE OF SIRACH 15:1~3

Sophia as Mother

Scripture

Therefore I prayed, and
    understanding was given me;
I called on God and the spirit of
    Sophia came to me.
I preferred Her to scepters and
    thrones,
and I accounted wealth as
    nothing in comparison with Her.
Neither did I liken to Her any
    priceless gem,
because all gold is but a little
    sand in Her sight,
and silver will be accounted as
    clay before Her.
I loved Her more than health and
    beauty,
and I chose to have Her rather
    than light,
because Her radiance never
    ceases.
All good things came to me
    along with Her,
and in Her hands accounted
    wealth.
I rejoiced in them all, because
    Sophia leads them;
but I did not know that She was
    their mother.
I learned without guile and I
    impart without grudging;
I do not hide Her wealth,
    for it is an unfailing treasure for mortals;
those who get it obtain
    friendship with God,
commended for the gifts that
    come from instruction.
(Wisdom 7:7-14, *NRSV*; I substituted *Sophia* for Wisdom)

They who reverence God will do this,
    and they who obey the law will encounter *Sophia.*
She will come to meet them like a
    mother, . . .
She will feed them with the bread of learning,
    and give them the water of wisdom to drink.

(Paraphrase of Sirach 15:1-3)

Questions for Personal Reflection or Group Discussion

1. *Sophia* is described as a mother in this scripture passage. In what ways has *Sophia* brought new growth in your life?

2. How could experiencing *Sophia's* mothering love affect your ability to nurture new life and be creative in your relationships and activities with others?

3. In what way have your foremothers nurtured you?

4. In what ways do you see yourself as a nurturer of others?

Prayer Suggestions

1. Find a quiet place where you can relax. Breathe deeply and slowly. Be aware of *Sophia's* mothering love for you. Open yourself to *Sophia* as She nurtures you in some special area, activity, or relationship.

2. Read the scripture passages above. Reread it as your personal prayer to *Sophia* as you experience new growth in your life.

3. Ask *Sophia* to help you be a nurturer of growth or birther of creativity in some new way in the lives of others. Listen to *Sophia's* response to you.

4. Picture women you know who express *Sophia's* mothering love by birthing new life in a physical, spiritual, emotional or intellectual way (mother, daughter, granddaughter, grandmother, great-grandmother, aunt, cousin, sister, friend etc.) Thank *Sophia* for the creative love each woman has shared with others.

5. Reflect on the stories of your foremothers as far back as you can go (mother, grandmothers, great grandmothers etc.) Create your own prayer to them. (e.g. "I thank you, for your wisdom and understanding, Mother; be here with me"; "I ask for your endurance and patience, Grandmother; walk with me through this crisis," etc.)

6. Make a list of your favorite spiritual foremothers (the women in the bible, women mystics and saints, contemporary women spiritual leaders) Next to each name write down their gifts. As you do this, thank *Sophia* for the ways these women reflect *Sophia's* mothering love.

7. Recall contemporary women who reflect *Sophia's* assertive mothering love in their work for justice, equality and human rights in the world. As you do this, thank *Sophia* for the ways these women image *Sophia*.

8. Contemplate yourself as a reflection of *Sophia's* mothering love. Spend time quietly rejoicing in the ways *Sophia* nurtures others through you. Be attentive of any thoughts, feelings, or insights these images stir up within you.

9. Record your feelings, images, thoughts, insights, decisions in a journal, poetry, art, song, dance or in some other creative way.

Sophia: Crucified Christ

Scripture

. . . but we proclaim Christ crucified, a stumbling block to Jews and foolishness to Gentiles, but to those who are called, both Jews and Greeks, Christ the power of God and wisdom (*Sophia*) of God. (1 Cor. 1: 23 *NRSV*)

Yet among the mature, we do speak wisdom, though it is not a wisdom of this age or of the rulers of this age, who are doomed to perish. But we speak God's wisdom (*Sophia*) secret and hidden, which God decreed before the ages for our glory. None of the rulers of this age understood this, for if they had, they would not have crucified the Lord of glory. (1 Cor. 2: 6-8 *NRSV*)

Questions for Personal Reflection or Group Discussion

1. What is the relationship between *Sophia* and the crucified Christ in these texts?

2. How do you feel about this relationship?

3. If you experience Christ crucified as *Sophia* what, if any, difference would this make in your life and/or in your relationship with Christ?

4. Do these scripture passages suggest any new images that could enrich your prayer?

Prayer Suggestions

1. Find a quiet place where you will not be interrupted. Focus on your breathing. Use the following exercise to help you center. Imagine yourself on the thirtieth floor of a skyscraper. Descend gradually to the first floor by counting slowly backward. 30 - 29 - 28, etc.

2. Read this scripture passage substituting *Sophia* for the word of wisdom.

3. Spend some time pondering this text. Contemplate Christ crucified as the wisdom (*Sophia*) of God. Simply, *be with* this divine mystery. Be aware of any new images or understandings of God that emerge from your reflection.

4. Read the story of the passion of Jesus Christ from one of the gospels. As you do so, substitute *Sophia* for Jesus. Be aware of

any differences this makes, any tensions or resistance that occur within you, and any new revelations or truths that you experience.

5. Image *Sophia* dying on the cross. Become present to Her suffering. Allow yourself to feel her pain, agony, loneliness. Do all you can to comfort her.

6. Reflect on your experience of the crucified *Sophia*. Be conscious of any thoughts, images, feelings that this encounter stirred up within you. Are you comfortable with this image of the crucified *Sophia*? Why? Why not?

7. Consider the difference your encounter with the crucified *Sophia* might make in your relationship with God and the impact this awareness might have on your life.

8. Share your response to this encounter with *Christ/Sophia*.

9. Record your feelings, images, thoughts, insights, decisions in a journal, poetry, art, song, dance or in some other creative way.

Jesus-Sophia: Healer of Our Stress

Scripture

"Come to me, all you who labor and weary, and are carrying heavy burdens, and I will give you rest. Take my yoke upon you, and learn from me; for I am gentle and humble in heart, and you will find rest for your souls. For my yoke is easy, and my burden is light." (Matthew 11:28-30 *NRSV*)

"put your neck under her yoke and let your souls receive instruction; it is to be found close by. (Sirach 51:26 *NRSV*)

"Bend your shoulders and carry her, and do not fret under her bonds. Come to her with you your soul, and keep her ways with all your might." (Sirach 6:25-26 *NRSV*)

Questions for Personal Reflection or Group Discussion

1. The Gospel of Matthew portrays Jesus speaking words like those of *Sophia*. How are the words of Jesus and *Sophia* alike?

2. How do you feel about Matthew's presentation of Jesus as *Sophia*?

3. What role do you think *Jesus-Sophia* will play in the development of a more inclusive Christ symbol?

4. In what way(s) could *Jesus-Sophia* be a healer of stress in your life?

Prayer Suggestions

1. Play some of your favorite, relaxing music. Let the beauty of the music wash over you like gentle waves refreshing your entire being.

2. Reflect upon areas of stress in your life. Make a list of these or draw a gift box and fill it with words or images that describe your stress.

3. You might want to write a dialogue with one or more of these stressors. After doing so, what did you discover about the source(s) of stress in your life. Consider any changes you might

want to make in your life-style to lessen or eliminate unnecessary stress. Think about healthier ways of coping with stress.

4. Reflect on times that you have experienced healing from anxiety or stress. Be aware of what you learned during these times about God, others and yourself. Offer thanks for these graced moments.

5. Image Jesus as *Sophia* incarnate present with you. Share your thoughts and feelings about one or more of the stressors that burden you at this time. Surrender these stresses to *Jesus-Sophia*. Imagine yourself resting in Her embrace. Open yourself to Her healing love. Listen to Her gentle Words. See yourself receiving whatever you need to live a more whole and peaceful life.

6. Remember people who have been channels of *Jesus-Sophia's* peace for you during stressful times. Offer thanks for them. Write a thank you to someone who has helped you during a difficult time in your life.

7. Remember people whom you have helped during stressful times. Pray for them. Write to or call someone who is experiencing anxiety in his/her life now.

8. Write your response to the above two suggestions on separate pieces of paper. Place them in a gift box. Each day, draw one out, pray for the people who need healing and offer thanks for those who have been instruments of peace in your life.

9. Record your feelings, images, thoughts, insights, decisions in a journal, poetry, art, song, dance or in some other creative way.

Women Prophets Persecuted

Scripture

Therefore also *Sophia* (the wisdom of God) said, 'I will send them prophets and apostles, some of whom they will kill and persecute.' (Luke 11:49 *NRSV*)

Questions for Personal Reflection or Group Discussion

1. Can you name women from the Judeo-Christian tradition whom you would select as mentors for women and men in our age? Why?

2. How do women today experience marginalization, discrimination and poverty?

3. Can you name contemporary women who reflect the image of *Jesus-Sophia* through their work for peace, justice, equality? Are there women prophets in your family? among your friends? community? neighborhood? city, country?

4. What impact have these courageous women had on your life? In what ways can you be a prophet?

Prayer Suggestions

1. In the stillness immerse yourself in the presence of *Jesus-Sophia*. Open yourself to the fullness of divine love. Be aware of any images that may come to you.

2. Find a picture of yourself and place it close to your prayer place. See yourself as a beautiful expression of the presence of *Jesus-Sophia*. As you do so, be aware of any thoughts, feelings, insights, or images that occur.

3. Reflect on your life. Recall the times you received and shared *Jesus-Sophia's* love . . . communicated divine values and promises . . . worked for peace, justice, truth, equality . . . labored for the coming of God's reign . . . acted as a contemporary prophet in our society.

4. Recall women today who suffer poverty, abuse, marginalization, discrimination, etc. Picture *Jesus-Sophia* touching their wounds and hurts with compassion. Imagine *Jesus-Sophia* empowering these women with the strength they need to change their lives. See them becoming contemporary prophets demon-

strating the way to transform unjust structures and social systems that cause human exploitation.

5. Remember women from the Judeo-Christian tradition who have been mentors for you. Ponder the rejection, suffering and persecution they experienced. How did these women courageously communicate God's values to God's people in spite of resistance and suffering? How does their witness enable you to do the same?

6. Select one or two women from the Judeo-Christian tradition whom you do not know. (Syncletica, Theodora, Maximilla, Prisca, Marcella, Perpetua, Felicitas, Dhuoda etc.). Get acquainted with them. How are they role models for women today? How are they role models for you today? Some helpful resources are: *Women of the Word* by Mary Lou Sleevi Ave Maria Press; *Silent Voices, Sacred Lives* by Barbara Bowe, Kathleen Hughes, Sharon Karam, Carolyn Osiek, Paulist Press, *The Women's Bible Commentary* by Carol A. Newsom and Sharon H. Ringe)

7. Reflect on women today who speak out for justice, truth, equality, peace in our world. Be aware of the rejection, suffering and persecution they undergo. Offer thanks for their example.

8. Be conscious of any new ways *Jesus-Sophia* may be calling you to be a contemporary prophet. Ask for the empowerment you will need to endure the sufferings that prophets face. Listen to *Jesus-Sophia's* response to you. Write down or verbalize your commitment to live as a prophet with a friend, spiritual companion, or community. Ask them for their support.

9. Record your feelings, images, thoughts, insights, decisions in a journal, poetry, art, song, dance or in some other creative way.

Jesus: Mirror of Sophia

Scripture

The Word was made flesh
and pitched her tent
among us.

      —John 1:14

(Translations from *Wisdom's Feast*)

Then the creator of all
things instructed me . . .
"Pitch your tent in Jacob,
Make Israel your inheritance."

      —Sirach 24:8

In the beginning was the Word,
and the Word was with God and
the Word was God. He was in
the beginning with God.

      —John 1:1-2

(Translations from *NRSV*)

With you is *Sophia* (wisdom),
she who knows your works
and was present when you
made the world . . .

      —Wisdom 9:9

Questions for Personal Reflection or Group Discussion

1. What similarities and differences do you find in these biblical passages?

2. How is Jesus a mirror of *Sophia*?

3. In what ways do you experience the unconditional acceptance of *Jesus-Sophia*?

4. In what ways do you mirror *Jesus-Sophia's* loving acceptance to others?

Prayer Suggestions

1. Make yourself comfortable. Look at your surroundings with wonder and awe like an infant seeing the world for the first time. As you do so, be aware of how each person/place/ thing reflects the beauty of *Jesus-Sophia*. Offer thanks for these "mirrors" of the divine in your life.

2. Notice the similarities between *Jesus and Sophia* in these Scripture passages. The Gospel of John identifies Jesus with *Sophia,* the pre-existent, co-creator. According to John, Jesus is *Sophia.* As you reflect on this mystery, be aware of any images or symbols that emerge.

3. Look into a mirror. Observe your body from head to toe. Affirm the beauty you see in your physical features. Accept any limitations that your body has. Notice any improvements you might

make. Write a dialogue with your body affirming your physical traits, features, or abilities. Apologize to your body for any neglect, ingratitude or abuse etc. Decide on one healthy, life-giving thing you will do for your body. After doing this, be aware of any new discoveries that you make about your body.

4. Now look into a mirror again. See *Jesus-Sophia* looking back at you. Listen as *Jesus-Sophia* expresses her loving acceptance of your whole being (body, mind, emotions, sexuality, spirituality etc.) Be aware of any obstacles within you to the unconditional acceptance of *Jesus-Sophia*. Surrender these obstacles to *Jesus-Sophia*. Rest in Her unconditional acceptance of you.

5. Draw a mandala or an image of *Jesus-Sophia's* unconditional love for you. To create this mandala, journey within yourself and wait patiently for a symbol, image or color to emerge that expresses *Jesus-Sophia's* loving acceptance of you. Place this in the center of the circle. Draw, paint, color the rest of the circle until it is finished. Reflect on the mandala you have created and write down any insights or intuitions that come to you.

6. Spend some time quietly contemplating yourself as a mirror of *Jesus-Sophia*. Offer thanks that you are a special, unique, irreplaceable reflection of *Jesus-Sophia*.

7. Reflect on new ways you can reflect *Jesus-Sophia's* loving acceptance of others in the ordinary activities of daily life. Ask *Jesus-Sophia* to help you show unconditional acceptance of others in your words and actions.

8. Decide on one thing you will say or do to mirror *Jesus-Sophia's* loving acceptance of another person. (e.g. forgive a hurt or insult, smile at someone you might otherwise ignore, listen to a chronic complainer, visit an elderly neighbor)

9. Record your feelings, images, thoughts, insights, decisions in a journal, poetry, art, song, dance or in some other creative way.

Sophia and the Woman Caught in Adultery

Scripture:

(This meditation puts *Sophia* into a Jesus story.)

Then each of them went home while *Sophia* went to the Mount of Olives. Early in the morning *Sophia* came again to the temple. All the people came to her and she sat down and began to teach them. The scribes and Pharisees brought a woman who had been caught in adultery; and making her stand before all of them, they said to her, "Teacher, this woman was caught in the very act of committing adultery. The law commands us to stone such a woman. Now what do you say?" They said this to test her, so that they might have some charge to bring against her. *Sophia* bent down and wrote with her finger on the ground. When they kept questioning her, she straightened up and said to them, "Let anyone among you who is without sin be the first to throw a stone at her." And once again she bent down and wrote on the ground. When they heard it, they went away, one by one, beginning with the elders; and *Sophia* was left alone with the woman standing before her. *Sophia* straightened up and said to her, "Woman, where are they? Has no one condemned you?" She said, "No one, has. And *Sophia* said, "Neither do I condemn you. Go your way, and from now on do not sin again."

(a retelling of John 8:53-9:11 adapted from *NRSV*)

Questions for Personal Reflection or Group Discussion

1. Does it make a difference to you whether Jesus or *Sophia* ministers to the woman caught in adultery?

2. How does *Sophia* relate to the woman caught in adultery? the scribes and Pharisees? you?

3. What would it be like to be the woman in this story? Would your life be changed in anyway after this encounter with *Sophia*?

4. What does *Sophia* want to communicate to you in this story?

Prayer Suggestions

1. Take several deep breaths. Feel each breath. . . . breathe in and out quietly. As you breathe in, say silently, "*Sophia*, you forgive me . . . deliver me . . . liberate me . . . heal me . . . As you

breathe out, say silently, "I am forgiven . . . liberated . . . delivered . . . healed . . .," etc.

2. Read the retelling of the woman caught in adultery. As you do so, imagine that you are present in the story. Describe the scene before the woman is introduced into this story. Listen to *Sophia* teach. What is *Sophia's* reaction to the scribes and Pharisees as they drag the woman caught in adultery before Her? How do you think the woman caught in adultery felt? How did the scribes and Pharisees react to *Sophia's* response:" "Let anyone among you who is without sin be the first to throw a stone at her. "How did the woman respond to *Sophia's* words: "Neither do I condemn you. Go your way, and from now on do not sin again."

3. Share with *Sophia* a time when you felt like either the Pharisees and scribes or the woman in the story. Open yourself to *Sophia's* extravagant love for you. As you do so, be aware of any thoughts, feelings, insights, images that emerge.

4. Reflect on you inner life. Ask *Sophia* to reveal to you areas in which you need to grow. What do you need to let go of? What do you need to change? Decide on one area on which you will focus. Share your decision with a spiritual friend, companion, or community. Invite them to support you in your efforts to grow spiritually.

5. Draw a circle on a piece of paper, try to identify some ways you have been unloving in your relationships with God, others, yourself. Write them down in the circle.

6. Be conscious of the consequences of your sinful choices. How has your attitudes and/ behavior hurt others and yourself? Ask *Sophia* to heal anyone you have hurt.

7. Confess your sins to *Sophia*. Ask for her forgiveness, deliverance and healing. Open yourself to *Sophia's* liberating healing love.

8. Ask *Sophia* to help you be more loving in the way you relate to those around you. Decide on at least one thing you will do to express love to those you have hurt in the past.

9. Record your feelings, images, thoughts, insights, decisions in a journal, poetry, art, song, dance or in some other creative way.

Part Three

The Feminine Divine in the Christian Tradition

Holy women and men throughout the ages have delighted in the Feminine Divine.[1] Three major themes emerge in the patristic and mystical literature of the Christian tradition: the Feminine Divine is portrayed as compassionate and tender; the Feminine Divine is nurturing and maternal; and the Feminine Divine is generative and sacrificial in her love. God is described in feminine and maternal imagery in the writings of the following mystics and saints. Using maternal language, Clement of Alexandria and John Chrysostom picture Christ as a mother nursing her child at her breast. Both Augustine of Hippo and Thomas Aquinas associate the biblical hen image found in Matthew's gospel with the wisdom of God, our mother. Albert the Great likewise describes the wisdom of God as the "first mother in whose womb we have been formed." The symbols associated with Brigit of Kildare as goddess reappear in the legends of her as Christian saint. Bernard of Clairvaux uses feminine imagery to portray the nurturing love of Christ and the pastoral responsibility of abbots and prelates. In a conversation Christ speaks to Mechtild von Hackeborn, a medieval mystic, and reveals to her that God's love is her mother and Christ is like the nursing mother who gives her child all the nourishment it needs for growth. Anselm of Canterbury speaks of Christ on the cross nourishing us with his blood. In Marguerite of Oingt's visions, Christ suffers labor pains on the cross in giving birth to the world. Hildegard of Bingen uses feminine imagery to refer to the Spirit, the Trinity and to describe Wisdom. In Hildegard's first vision, the Feminine Divine appears as a radiant woman worshipped by angels. According to Julian of Norwich there is no relationship which more perfectly reflects the love of God than maternal love. Her *Revelations of Divine Love* provide the most comprehensive theological development of the Motherhood of God in the Christian tradition. Although traces of the maternity of God can be found in the work of Bridget of Sweden and Catherine of Siena, none speak in trinitarian terms with Julian's clarity and harmony. Julian speaks of the characteristics of Divine Motherhood expressed in imagery which is inclusive, warm, embracing and accepting. According to Julian, Divine Motherhood is related to compassion and brings about compassionate living. It involves birthing and all the labor associated with birthing; since all creatures are birthed by God, God is revealed in all creation. In

---

1.   In my research on metaphors for the Feminine Divine in the Christian tradition, I found Jennifer Heimmel's dissertation an outstanding source: *"God is Our Mother": Julian of Norwich and the Medieval Image of Christian Feminine Divinity*. New York: St John's University, 1980.

Julian's words: "I understand three ways of contemplating the motherhood in God. the first is the foundation of our nature's creation; the second is his taking of our nature, where the motherhood of grace begin; the third is the motherhood of work. And in that by the same grace, everything is penetrated, in length and in breadth, in height and in depth without end; and is all one love . . . I am . . . the power and goodness of the fatherhood. I am . . ., the wisdom and lovingness of the motherhood. I am . . ., the light and grace which is all blessed love. I am . . . , the Trinity. I am . . ., the Unity." (Julian of Norwich, *Showings*, ed. Edmund Colledge et al. (New York: Paulist, 1978 pp. 293-299.)

In this section you are invited to contemplate the rich treasury of feminine images and delight in the Feminine Divine with the following great men and women of faith: Clement of Alexandria, John Chrysostom, Augustine of Hippo, Bridget of Kildare, Bernard of Clairvaux, Anslem of Canterbury, Hildegard of Bingen, Thomas Aquinas, Albert the Great, Marguerite of Oingt, Mechtild von Hackeborn, and Julian of Norwich.

Clement of Alexandria

After the Bible the next reference to a feminine maternal God is found in the second century patristic writings of Clement of Alexandria (150-215 A.D.) In his treatise "The Rich Man's Salvation" Clement, uses the imagery of nourishing and suckling the infant to describe the love of Mother God. Clement shares his vision of God in the following words: "God in his very self is love . . . And while the unspeakable part of Him is Father, the part that has sympathy with us is Mother. By His loving the Father became of woman's nature." [Source: *Clement of Alexandria*, trans. G.W. Butterworth Cambridge, Mass: Harvard University Press, 1953, p. 347.] By His loving the Father became of woman's nature." He affirms the sexual equality of the divinity: "The Word is everything to His little ones, both father and mother, educator and nurse." [Source: Clement of Alexandria, *Christ the Educator*, The Fathers of the Church, No. 23, trans Simon P. Wood (New York: Fathers of the Church Inc., 1954) p. 40. In *Paidagogos* Clement devotes one chapter to a lengthy, comprehensive explanation of a suckling nurturing God. He uses female images describing Christ as "milk" our perfect spiritual food. He refers to "God, the Nourisher" of the "re-created, reborn child." [Source: Clement of Alexandria, *Christ the Educator*, p. 39].

God the Nourisher

"I am your nurse
giving Myself for bread,
which none who taste have any longer trial of death,
and giving day by day drink of immortality."

(*Clement of Alexandria*, trans. G.W. Butterworth, Cambridge, Mass.: Harvard University Press, 1953) p. 319.

John Chrysostom

John Chrysostom (347-407 A.D.) renowned orator and patriarch of Constantinople uses maternal imagery to describe God's nourishing love in several passages of his writings. In his *Homilies on the Gospel of Saint Matthew* John quotes Matthew and uses the scriptural image of God as mother hen: "And His affection He indicates by the similitude; for indeed the creature is warm in its love towards its brood. And everywhere in the prophets is this same image of the wings, and in the song of Moses and in the Psalms, indicating His great protection and care." [Source: John Chrysostom, *Homilies on the Gospel of Saint Matthew*, The Nicene and Post Nicenen Fathers, No. 10 1st ser., ed. Philip Schaff (Grand Rapids, Michigan: Wm. B. Eerdmans Publishing Co., 1956), p. 447. In "Homily 82" of the same series on the gospel of Matthew John compares the nourishment to the child from the human mother with that of God: "What shepherd feeds his sheep with his own limbs? And why do I say shepherd? There are often mothers who after the travail of birth send out their children to other women as nurses; but He endureth not to do this, but Himself feeds us with His own blood, and by all means entwines us with Himself." [Source: John Chrysostom, *Homilies on the Gospel of Saint Matthew*, The Nicene and Post Nicene Fathers, No. 10. 1st ser, ed. Philip Schaff (Grand Rapids, Michigan: Wm. B. Eerdmans Publishing Co., 1956) p. 495-96. Likewise in his discourse on Baptismal instructions, John uses maternal imagery. "Have you seen with what food he nurtures us all? It is by the same food that we have been formed and fed. Just as a woman nurtures her offspring with her own blood and milk, so also Christ continuously nurtures with His own blood those whom He has begotten." [Source: John Chrysostom, *Baptismal Instructions*, trans. Paul W. Harkins, Ancient Christian Writers, No. 31, eds. Johannes Quasten and Joseph C. Plumpe (Westminster, Maryland, Newman Bookshop, 1963) pp. 55-56.

Eucharist as Nourishment

"See ye not the infants with how much eagerness they lay hold of the breast? With what earnest desire they fix their lips upon the nipple? With the like let us also approach this table, and the nipple of the spiritual cup. Or rather, with much more eagerness, let us, as infants at the breast, draw out the grace of the spirit, let it be our one sorrow, not to partake of this food."

(Source: John Chrysostom, *Homilies on the Gospel of Saint Matthew,* The Nicene and Post Nicene Fathers, No. 10. 1st ser, ed. Philip Schaff (Grand Rapids, Michigan: Wm. B. Eerdmans Publishing Co., 1956) p. 495-496.

Questions for Personal Reflection or Group Discussion

1. Both Clement of Alexandria and John Chrysostom use maternal imagery to describe God the Nourisher. Does this imagery appeal to you? Why? Why not?

2. If you wanted to describe God's nourishing love today, what symbols or images would you use?

3. How is the Eucharist a symbol of God's nourishing love for you?

4. In what ways is the Christian community a reflection of the divine Nourisher?

Prayer Suggestions

1. Find a quiet place and become comfortable. Relax in the presence of God, the Nourisher. Imagine an infant being nourished on his/her Mother's breast. Allow this image to speak to you of God's nourishing love.

2. Read the passage from Clement of Alexandria as if God, the Nourisher is speaking to you. Be aware of any thoughts, feelings, images, insights that emerge as you do so.

3. Read the passage of John Chrysostom. Image yourself as a mother. (Men, try this.) In your imagination picture yourself holding your infant in your arms . . . delighting in your baby . . . playfully caressing your infant . . . breast-feeding your baby. Be aware of any maternal feelings that you experience.

4. Draw an image or a mandala of God nourishing you. Choose an image or symbol of God's nourishing love in your life. Begin by

reflecting on memories from your past when you experienced God as your Nourisher . . . feeding you with divine nourishment. Then draw your mandala.

5. God gave us bread from heaven that we might become bread for the world. Be aware of ways in which you are a reflection of the divine Nourisher to others. How do you feed the poor and the stranger? How do nourish those in need of understanding and compassion? How can you become bread for the world?

6. Pray "give us this day our daily bread" as a mantra asking the divine Nourisher to provide nourishment for those who suffer from physical and spiritual hungers throughout the world. Decide on something you can do to alleviate the hunger of others in the world. Some examples are: cook a meal once a month or collect canned food and clothing for a local shelter, give money to a overseas emergency relief organization, join a lobbying group such as Bread for the World to create laws, change policies to help the poor etc.

7. Next time you celebrate the Eucharist, be aware of the areas of your life in which you hunger and thirst for God. Open yourself to receive the divine nourishment you need from the body of Christ. As you listen to the Word . . . receive the nourishment you need. As you worship in the assembly . . . receive the nourishment you need. As you eat and drink the sacred meal . . . receive the nourishment you need. As you go forth . . . share the nourishment you have received with others.

8. The Eucharist is a communal meal that nourishes us with the Body of Christ so that we become the Body of Christ broken and shared for God's people. The Christian community gathered around the eucharistic table is called to be a reflection of the divine Nourisher to the world. Offer thanks for the ways your Christian community gives nourishment to others, especially the poor and needy. Reflect on the role of the Christian community, the Body of Christ, to be a source of nourishment for a world that has so many hungers. Offer thanks for the ways you are the Body of Christ to others.

9. Record your feelings, images, thoughts, insights, decisions in a journal, poetry, art, song, dance or in some other creative way.

Brigit of Kildare

The myth of Brigit describes her journey from Mother Goddess to Irish saint. The symbols associated with Brigit's role as goddess reappear in her legends as a Christian saint. "The images of milk, fire, sun, serpents are common in stories of St. Brigit," observes scholar Mary Condren, "while the themes of compassion, generosity, hospitality, spinning, weaving, smithwork, healing, and agriculture run throughout her various "Lives." Her sacred objects, her mantle, hair, and holy wells were take over into her Christian devotional forms." [Henry Foster McClintock, "The Mantle of St. Brigid at Bruge," *Journal of the Royal Society of Antiquaries of Ireland*, 7th ser., 66, no 5 (1936):32-40 cited by Mary Condren, *The Serpent And The Goddess,* San Francisco: Harper & Row, 1989, p. 65-66] According to Celtic stories, fifth century Saint Bridget healed the sick, made the dumb speak, protected the harvest, turned water into ale, defended the rights of the poor, fostered learning and founded a order of nuns in Kildare. The "Lives of Brigit," perhaps a little embarrassed by the story, describe her episcopal ordination with tongue and cheek Irish wit: "The bishop being intoxicated with the grace of God did not recognize what he was reciting from his book, for he consecrated Brigit with the orders of a bishop.' This virgin alone in Ireland," said Mel, "will hold the episcopal ordination.' While she was being consecrated a fiery column ascended from her head." [*Bethu Brigte*, ed. Donncha O hAodha (Dublin:Institute for Advanced Studies, 1978 p. 24) cited in *The Serpent and the Goddess* p. 76.] In a medieval church at Killinaboy Brigit's image a *sheela-na-igg* (a figure holding the entrance to her womb wide open) is carved on the top of the arch to the door, inviting the community to enter the church through her "womb." (Cf. Liam de Paor, "Saint Mac Creiche of Liscannor," *Eriu* 30 (1979):93-121,119. cited in *The Serpent And The Goddess* p. 65)

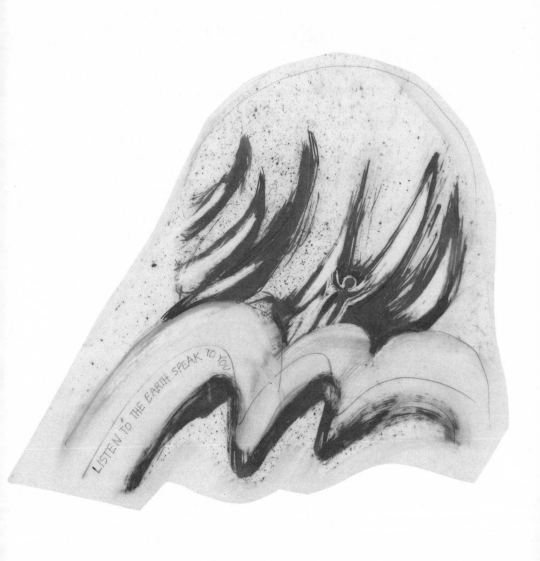

Mother Goddess and Christian Saint

Brigit was born at sunrise neither within nor without a house, was bathed in milk, her breath revives the dead, a house in which she is staying flames up to heaven, cow-dung blazes before her, oil is poured on her head; she is fed from the milk of a white red-eared cow; a fiery pillar rises over her head; sun rays support her wet cloak; she remains a virgin; and she was one of the two mothers of Christ the Anointed.

(Source: Wh. Stokes, *Three Middle Irish Homilies on the Lives of SS. Patrick, Brigit, and Columcille* (Calcutta: privately printed, 1877) cf. also *Lives of Saints from the Book of Lismore*, Anecdota Oxoniensia Medieval and Modern Series no. 5 (Oxford: Clarendon Press, 1890), p. 199.)*

In a medieval church at Killinaboy her image a *sheela-na-gig* (a figure holding the entrance to her womb wide open) is carved on the top of the arch to the door, inviting the community to enter the church through her "womb."

. (Cf. Liam de Paor, "Saint Mac Creiche of Liscannor,: *Eriu* 30 (1979):93-121,119.)*

*(Both quotes are found in Mary Condren, *The Serpent And The Goddess*, San Francisco: Harper & Row, 1989 p. 65)

Questions for Personal Reflection or Group Discussion

1. Brigit as Mother Goddess is described as a a "activist mother," outraged at the violence and rape which her children suffer. Mary Condren comments on one of Brigit's symbols and roles as Mother Goddess: "The Sacred Cow symbolized the sacredness of motherhood: through her milk the life-force itself was sustained and nourished. By no means a passive giver of milk, she was an active mother fighting for the health, safety, and well-being of her offspring. Brigit as Mother Goddess at all times appears as the woman who mourns for the fate of her children and who is particularly outraged by plunder and rape." [Lebor Gabala Erenn, ed. R.A.S. MacAlister, (Dublin: Irish Texts Society, nos. 34, 35, 39, 41, 44, 1938-56). pt 4, p. 159, cited in *The Serpent and the Goddess*, p. 58.]

Have you ever felt indignation at the violence and human rights abuses directed against women, children, people with disabilities, the elderly, homosexuals, etc. in our society/culture? in other societies/ cultures where people suffer poverty and oppression on a daily basis? What can we do to resolve some of these problems in our times? Is there anything you can do to help?

2. Which, if any, of the images describing Brigit in these passages do you find meaningful? powerful? energizing? liberating? Why?

3. The womb has often been used in the Christian tradition as a baptismal image. Why do you think the womb symbol of Brigit on the church door was an important maternal image for the Celtic people?

Why do you think the womb is an powerful symbol of baptism for Christians today?

4. How does Brigit as Mother Goddess and Christian Saint reflect God's womb love for all creation?

Prayer Suggestions

1. Begin by getting in a comfortable position and closing your eyes. Slowly take a few deep breaths. Be aware of the air flowing through your nostrils as you breathe in and out. Allow your body to relax.

2. Open yourself to the imagery of Brigit. As you read these passages, be aware of any images that appeal to your imagination. Choose one of these images to contemplate on a deeper level.

3. Allow a picture to form in your imagination that expresses the spiritual power of Brigit. (e.g. For some today Brigit is an important symbol of the empowerment of women in a patriarchal society and church.) Draw or paint a mandala or create a symbol of Brigit that relates to you. You may wish to play Celtic music in the background as you paint or draw your mandala, mold clay, do needle point, weave cloth, etc.

4. As you look at the mandala or image you created, breathe in the spirit of Brigit that radiates from the mandala or image. Let it fill you with a deep sense of your own mystery . . . your own depths . . . your own hopes . . . your own dreams . . . your own wholeness . . . etc. You may wish to express your feelings in song or dance.

5. If you wish, and if it is appropriate enter into a dialogue with Brigit about one or two major issues in women's lives . . . women's experiences . . . empowerment . . . love . . . equality . . . connection . . . healing . . . justice . . . liberation, etc.

6. Now share with Brigit your concern for victims of rape. . . violence . . . abuse . . . crimes of hate . . . human rights violations. etc. directed against women, children, people with disabilities, the elderly, homosexuals, etc. . . . in our society/culture . . . in other societies/cultures. Express your fears, anger, outrage, guilt, helplessness, hopes, about this situation with Brigit. Be aware of anything you can do to help victims of violent crime and/or to prevent crime in your area. (some opportunities to reach out include the following: women's shelters, victims' support group, rape hot line, neighborhood watch, anti-crime groups, human rights groups etc.)

7. Reflect on the "womb" as a powerful symbol of baptism. As babies come forth from the waters of the womb, and are embraced by their parents, the newly baptized are lifted up from the baptismal waters, and welcomed by the members of the community. As a baby is born from the darkness of the watery womb so in baptism we die to the darkness of sin and death and rise with Christ from the baptismal pool, the church's watery womb, as new creations. Offer thanks for your baptism.

8. Contemplate the earth enveloped in the eternal mystery of God's womb love inviting you to hear the voices of the trees . . . mountains . . . the oceans . . . the earth . . . the animals . . . flowers . . . plants etc. Listen to the earth speak to you through a golden-red sunrise . . . polluted air . . . a gentle cool breeze . . . damaging oil spills . . . gentle lambs . . . extinct wild life . . . the sparkling water of a lake . . . vanishing rain forests . . . the lush, green grass . . . the hole in the ozone. etc. Be aware of how Brigit as Mother Goddess and Christian Saint reflects God's womb love for all creation. Conduct a dialogue with Brigit sharing your feelings and thoughts with her. Do something concrete to express your gratitude for creation. (Plant a flower, sow seed, weed a garden, pet an animal etc.)

9. Record your feelings, images, thoughts, insights, decisions in a journal, poetry, art, song, dance or in some other creative way.

Augustine of Hippo, Thomas Aquinas, Albert the Great, and Julian of Norwich

Introduction:

Augustine of Hippo (354-430 A.D.), a renowned Patristic bishop and doctor of the church refers to the feminine aspects of God in his writings. In several places, Augustine uses Matthew's biblical image of God as mother hen:

> "Let us put our egg under the wings of that Hen of the Gospel, which crieth out to that false and abandoned city, 'O Jerusalem, how often would I have gathered thy children together, even as a hen her chickens, and thou wouldest not!' Let it not be said to us 'How often would I, and thou wouldest not!' For that hen is the Divine Wisdom." [Source: St. Augustine, *Sermons on the Mount, Harmony of the Gospels, Homilies on the Gospels*, A Select Library of Nicene and Post Nicene Fathers, Vol. VI, 1st ser., ed. Philip Schaff (Grand Rapids, Michigan: Wm. B. Eerdmans Publishing Co. 1956), p. 434.]

Augustine clearly associates this maternal image found in Matthew's gospel with the wisdom of God, which he calls "our Mother." Augustine's other reference to God as nourishing mother describes the wisdom of God as milk:

> "He who has promised us heavenly food has nourished us on milk, having recourse to a mother's tenderness. For just as a mother, suckling her infant, transfers from her flesh the very same food which otherwise would be unsuited to a babe . . . so our Lord, in order to convert His wisdom into milk for our benefit, came to us clothed in flesh. It is the Body of Christ, then, which here says: 'And thou shalt nourish me'" [Source: St. Augustine, *On the Psalms*, trans, Dame Scholastica Hebgin and Dame Felicitas Corrigan, Ancient Christian Writers, No. 30, eds. Johannes Quasten and Walter Burghardt (Westminister, Maryland, Newman Press, 1961), II, 20-21.]

Similarly, Thomas Aquinas (1225-1274), one of the greatest theologians and doctors of the church applies the biblical hen image to the wisdom of God: concluding "the wisdom of God" (is) "thus indeed, our mother." [Source Santi Thomae Aquinatis, *Quatuor Evangelia*, Vol. XI of *Opera Omnia* (New York: Musurgia

Publishers, 1949), I, 268., translated from Latin by Rev. Michael Pollitt]

Albert the Great (1200-1280), a doctor of the church, likewise, refers to the wisdom of God as the "first mother in whose womb we have been formed." Albert speaks of the breasts of this divine mother of wisdom who is more than a mother who formed and carried us in the light of foreknowledge. [Source: Alberti Magni, *Postilla Super Isaiam*, Vol. 19, *Opera Omnia* ed. Ferdinandus Siepmann (Aschendorff: Monasterii Westfalorum, 1952) pp. 626-27, 491, cited in Heimmel, pp. 27-28]

Like Augustine, Thomas Aquinas, Albert the Great and others, Julian of Norwich, the fourteenth century anchoress and mystic, affirms repeatedly that the wisdom of God is our mother, as in "And the deep wisdom of the Trinity is our Mother, in whom we are enclosed."

(Source: Trans. Edmund Colledge and James Walsh. *Julian of Norwich: Showings* Classics of Western Spirituality, New York: Paulist Press, 1978, chapter 54, p. 285)

The Wisdom of God as Our Mother

Augustine of Hippo

"He who has promised us heavenly food has nourished us on milk, having recourse to a mother's tenderness. For just as a mother, suckling her infant, transfers from her flesh the very same food which otherwise would be unsuited to a babe . . . so our Lord, in order to convert His wisdom into milk for our benefit, came to us clothed in flesh. It is the Body of Christ, then, which here says: 'And thou shalt nourish me'."

[Source: St. Augustine, *On the Psalms,* trans, Dame Scholastica Hebgin and Dame Felicitas Corrigan, Ancient Christian Writers, No. 30, eds. Johannes Quasten and Walter Burghardt (Westminister, Maryland, Newman Press, 1961), II, 20-21.]

Thomas Aquinas

"the wisdom of God, (is) thus indeed, our mother."

[Source Santi Thomae Aquinatis, *Quatuor Evangelia*, Vol. XI of *Opera Omnia* (New York: Musurgia Publishers, 1949), I, 268, translated from Latin by Rev. Michael Pollitt]

Albert the Great

Wisdom is the "first mother in whose womb we have been formed"

[Source: Alberti Magni, *Postilla Super Isaiam*, Vol. 19, *Opera Omnia* ed. Ferdinandus Siepmann (Aschendorff: Monasterii Westfalorum, 1952) pp. 626-27 quoted in Jennifer Perone Heimmel, *"God is Our Mother" Julian of Norwich and the Medieval Image of Christian Feminine Divinity*, New York: St. John's University, 1980 dissertation, pp. 27-28]

Julian of Norwich

"And the deep wisdom
of the Trinity is our Mother,
in whom we are enclosed."

(Source: Trans. Edmund Colledge and James Walsh. *Julian of Norwich: Showings* Classics of Western Spirituality, New York: Paulist Press, 1978, chapter 54, p. 285) chapter 54, p. 285)

Questions for Personal Reflection or Group Discussion

1. What does it mean to be a daughter or son of the Wisdom of God (Sophia)?

2. How do you need the Wisdom of God (Sophia) to be a mother to you?

3. What do you think the Wisdom of God (Sophia) is communicating today through her womb love for you? for those you love? for those you don't like? for all creation?

4. What word, symbol or image best describes your experience of the Wisdom of God (Sophia) as your Mother?

Prayer Suggestions

1. Spend a little time in stillness. Close your eyes. Relax your body. Concentrate on slow, deep breathing. Picture yourself surrounded by the presence of divine Wisdom (Sophia). Soak in Her presence as you would a warm bath. Allow Sophia to enfold you in Her womb love.

2. Become aware that the Wisdom of God (Sophia) is your Mother. In memory and imagination allow yourself to experience Her fully. Be conscious of any thoughts, feelings, sensations, insights, intuitions that emerge during this encounter.

3. Image yourself . . . your family . . . your community . . . people you love . . . people you don't like . . . the earth . . . all creation coming forth from the womb of divine Wisdom. How does this birthing experience feel? What words, symbols or images might describe the continual birthing process of life each day from Her womb?

4. Be conscious of any new understandings Wisdom (Sophia) is revealing to you through Her ongoing birthing activity of creation. How is this different than what you have been traditionally taught?

5. Enter into the mind and heart of your Mother, the Wisdom of God (Sophia). Ask Her to reveal your gifts and strengths. Look at Sophia and listen to Her as She proudly names your gifts. Afterwards, write down these good things about yourself. Offer thanks for these gifts.

6. Create a litany of praise to the Wisdom of God (Sophia) your Mother.

"Wisdom, nurturing womb of creation, I sing your praises."

"Sophia, mother of justice, I glorify you."

"Sophia, pregnant with Mystery, I contemplate your presence."

"Wisdom, activist mother, I celebrate your passion."

7. Compose a contemporary psalm expressing your feelings openly and honestly to the Wisdom of God (Sophia) your Mother.

8. Draw a mandala. Begin by opening yourself to the Wisdom of God (Sophia), your Mother. Get in touch with Her knowledge, wisdom, truth, justice, peace, assertiveness, passion, etc. Invite Sophia to reveal Herself to you as Mother. When you are ready, fill your circle with colors, symbols, and /or images of Her presence in your life.

9. Record your feelings, thoughts, insights decisions in a journal, poetry, art, song, dance or in some other creative way.

Anselm of Canterbury

Anselm of Canterbury (1033-1109) uses maternal imagery to describe both Paul and Jesus as "mothers by your affection . . . mothers by your kindness . . . mothers by your mercy." [Source: St. Anselm, *The Prayers and Meditations of St. Anselm*. Trans. Sr. Benedicta Ward. Middlesex, England: Penguin Books Inc., 1973, p. 154. Anselm prays that the soul of the sinner be placed "at the feet of Christ, your mother . . . for Christ is even more his mother" and prays, "Do, mother of my soul, what the mother of my flesh would do." (Source St. Anselm, *The Prayers and Meditations of St. Anselm*. Trans. Sr. Benedicta Ward. Middlesex, England: Penguin Books Inc., 1973, p. 155.

In his prayer *Oratio 10* Anselm calls Paul "nurse" and "mother" ". . . You [Paul] are among Christians like a nurse who not only cares for her children but also gives birth to them a second time by the solicitude of her marvelous love." Anslem compares the comforting, mothering Jesus to a hen gathering her chicks under her wing (Matt. 23:37) ". . . but you, Jesus, good lord, are you not also a mother? Are you not that mother who, like a hen, collects her chickens under her wings? Truly, master, you are a mother. For what others have conceived and given birth to, they have received from you . . . You are the author, others are the minister. It is then you, above all, Lord God, who are mother." (Caroline Walker Bynum, *Jesus as Mother*, Berkeley: University of California Press, 1982. pp. 113-114)

Jesus as Mother

But you too, good Jesus, are you not also a mother?

Are you not a mother who like a hen gathers her chicks beneath
   her wings? . . .

and you, my soul, dead in yourself,

run under the wings of Jesus your mother

and lament your griefs under his feathers.

Ask that your wounds may be healed

and that, comforted, you may live again.

Christ, my mother, you gather your chickens under your wings;

This dead chicken of yours puts himself under your wings . . .

Warm your chicken, give life to your dead one, justify your
   sinner.

Anselm of Canterbury ("Prayer to St. Paul," *The Prayers and
Meditations of St. Anselm,* trans. S. Benedicta Ward (New York:
Penguin Books, 1973) 153-56; amended for inclusivity in *She
Who Is* p. 150.

Questions for Personal Reflection or Group Discussion

1. Anslem portrays the comforting, nurturing Jesus as a hen
gathering her chicks under her wing (Matt. 23:37) and suggests
that mother Jesus revive his spiritual life. Are there any obstacles
that you are facing in your spiritual journey now?

2. If so, are you aware of the comforting, nurturing love of Jesus for you in your struggle? What was this like for you? If not,
what prevented you from being aware of Jesus' comforting, nurturing love?

3. How have you shared the comforting, nurturing love with
others during times of struggle?

4. What do you need to do now to nurture your own spiritual
life especially in areas where you are encountering some difficulty
or struggle?

Prayer Suggestions

1. Become still by breathing deeply and slowly for several minutes. Use the following exercise to center. Imagine a mother hen gathering her chicks under her wing . . . Watch the chicks as they walk close by her side, chirping softly . . . See the mother hen looking around her at the chicks on their morning barnyard stroll . . . Now observe what happens when a large dog barking loudly approaches the chicks . . . Notice how she spreads her wings, trying to gather her chicks close to her . . . Cackling loudly the mother hen protests this intrusion and scoots with her chicks to safety through the hen-house door.

2. As you read Anselm's reflection, think about the ways you have experienced comforting, nurturing love during difficult situations in your life. Who are the people who nurtured you during these times? What events or relationships caused the struggle or difficulty? In what ways did you grow spiritually as a result of this struggle or difficulty? Were you aware of Jesus' comforting, nurturing love present with you? Did you feel warm, safe, and secure? If not, what prevented your from being aware of Jesus' comforting, nurturing love? Does Anselm's image of Jesus as mother hen remind you of God's comforting, nurturing care? Share your response to these questions with Jesus, your nurturing mother.

3. Draw a mandala. Begin by opening yourself to the comforting, nurturing love of Jesus. Let that love permeate your entire being. Reflect on areas of struggle in your life. Get in touch with the nurturing spirit of Jesus deep within you. Allow that love to comfort, embrace and strengthen you in these areas. When you are ready, fill your circle with colors, symbols, and/or images of Jesus' comforting, nurturing presence in your life.

4. Write a prayer expressing your feelings to Jesus for the comforting, nurturing love you have felt especially during times of struggle and difficulty.

5. Call or write to someone who has helped you through difficult times. Express your gratitude to them for the ways he/she comforted or nurtured you.

6. Be aware of ways in which you have shared the comforting, nurturing love with others during their times of struggle and difficulty. Thank Jesus for these opportunities to love others.

7. Be conscious of ways you can nurture your spiritual growth by being good to yourself. What have you done for yourself to be-

come a more holy and whole person? Do you eat balanced meals, get plenty of rest, take time for solitude and relaxation, avoid excess work or stress etc.? Dialogue with Jesus about these opportunities for spiritual growth.

8. Choose one way you will be good to yourself in the next day. Do it.

9. Record your feelings, images, thoughts, insights, decisions in a journal, poetry, art, song, dance or in some other creative way.

St. Bernard of Clairvaux

Use of maternal imagery to describe God and Christ appears to have been popular in the twelfth century in the works of men: the Cistercian monks Bernard of Clairvaux (1153), Guerric of Igny (1157), Aelred of Rievaulx (1167), Isaac of Stella (1169), Adam of Perseigne (1221), Helinand of Froidmont (1235), and William of St. Thierry (1148) The meaning of mother-Jesus in the twelfth-century affective spirituality of the Cistercians is compassion, nurturing, and union. Bernard of Clairvaux also uses maternal imagery to describe Jesus, Moses, Peter, Paul, abbots, prelates and himself as an abbot. To Bernard, maternal imagery does not refer to giving birth, conceiving or sheltering in the womb but rather nurturing, specifically suckling. "Breasts, to Bernard," observes scholar Caroline Walker Bynum, "are a symbol of the pouring out to others of affectivity or of instruction and almost invariably suggest to him a discussion of the duties of prelates or abbots." (Bynum, *Jesus as Mother,* p. 115) To Abbot Baldwin of Rieta Bernard writes: "As a mother loves her only son, so I loved you when you clung to my side pleasing my heart." (Letter 201, PL 182: col. 369B-C, cited in Bynum, *Jesus as Mother*, p. 116)

YOUR
BREASTS
ARE
BETTER
THAN
WINE
SMELLING
SWEET
OF
THE
BEST
OINTMENTS.
SONG 1:1-2

Jesus as Mother and the Abbot as Mother

In his sermon on the *Song of Songs* Bernard explains the references to breasts in the scripture passage in this way:

> Commenting on the verse "For your breasts are better than wine, smelling sweet of the best ointments" (Song 1:1-2), Bernard first associates nursing with Christ the bridegroom: "She [the bride, i.e., the soul] would seem to say to the bridegroom [Christ]: 'What wonder if I presume to ask you for this favor, since your breasts have given me such overwhelming joy?' . . . When she said, then, 'Your breasts are better than wine,' she meant: "The richness of the grace that flows from your breasts contributes far more to my spiritual progress than the biting reprimands of superiors."

In this sermon also, Bernard uses maternal imagery to describe the pastoral responsibility of the abbot:

> . . . how many [of them] there are today who reveal their lack of the requisite qualities . . . They display an insatiable passion for gains . . . Neither the peril of souls nor their salvation gives them any concern. They are certainly devoid of the maternal instinct. . . . There is no pretense about a true mother, the breasts that she displays are full for the taking. She knows how to rejoice with those who rejoice, and to be sad with those who sorrow [Rom 12:15], pressing the milk of encouragement without intermission from the breast of joyful sympathy, the milk of consolation from the breast of compassion. (Sermon 10, par. 3 OB 1:49-50; trans. Walsh, *Song* 1:62-62 quoted in Caroline Walker Bynum *Jesus as Mother* pp. 117-118)

Questions for Personal Reflection or Group Discussion

1. To Bernard, breasts are a powerful symbol of Christ's nurturing love. What feelings are evoked in you by this maternal image?

2. Bernard uses breasts to symbolize the maternal ministry of the abbot. Do you think it is important for spiritual leaders today to be nurturing in order to fulfill their pastoral responsibilities in the community? Why? Why not?

3. Do you believe that God will nurture you with whatever you need to become the person you are called to be?

4. What symbol or image would you choose to describe God's nurturing love in your life?

Prayer Suggestions

1. Begin by becoming still. Breathe slowly, gently, deeply. Open yourself to God's nurturing love flowing through every area of your body. Invite God to "mother" you in some new way. Allow yourself to *feel* this love as it permeates your entire being.

2. Reflect on several occasions in which you experienced nurturing love. Did you *feel* loved by God on these occasions? What way(s) did you grow as a result of these experiences? Are you a different person today because of these experiences? Why? Why not?

3. Become aware of a part of yourself that needs to be nurtured. Imagine this part of yourself as a "character" in a book. Look . . . listen . . . be aware of his/her physical characteristics, mental abilities . . . feelings . . . gifts . . . limitations . . . needs. etc. Conduct a conversation with this "character." Picture yourself loving this "character" with motherly love. What happens? What difference does it make? In what ways does your "mothering" affect this part of yourself? How does it change how you *feel* about this part of yourself?

4. Reflect on Bernard's use of breasts as symbols of Christ's nurturing love. What feelings are evoked in you by this maternal image? Recall a person who gave you nurturing love recently. Be aware of your *feelings* about this experience. What symbol or image would you use to describe your *feelings* about this experience? Draw, write, create, make this symbol or image. Place this symbol in an important place. When you look at this symbol, remember how it *felt* to be nurtured, offer thanks, and open yourself to being nurtured on a deeper level.

5. Bernard uses breasts to describe the nurturing role of the abbot. Recall spiritual leaders who are reflections of the nurturing, compassionate love of God in their ministry to the community. Be aware of any *feelings* that emerge when you reflect on their spiritual leadership. Offer thanks for their maternal love.

6. Picture God nurturing you right now with whatever you need to be who you are called to be. Be aware of any *feelings* that emerge as you do so. Create a mantra reflecting your *feelings*

about this experience of divine maternal love. Recite this mantra throughout the day as a reminder of God's motherly love for you. Some examples of mantras are: "Mother, I delight in you." "Sophia, I am joyful . . . peaceful . . . strong . . . loving. etc."

7. Take a walk. Be as fully present to God's nurturing presence in creation as possible. Invite God to "mother" you through the beauty of flowers, trees, clouds, sun, rain, bees, cats, dogs, squirrels, birds, roses, daisies, wind, cold, frost, etc. Offer thanks to Mother God for loving you through mother earth.

8. Take a walk. Be aware of yourself as a reflection of God's maternal love. As you walk, bless everything you hear, see, touch, feel, taste with Mother God's nurturing love.

9. Record your feelings, images, thoughts, insights, decisions in a journal, poetry, art, song, dance or in some other creative way.

Mechtild von Hackeborn

Mechtild von Hackeborn (d. 1298), a medieval mystical writer describes the motherhood of God in her writings. In her *Liber Specialis Gratiae,* the record of her revelations and conversations with God, Mechtild refers to both Christ and the Holy Spirit as mother. When she is upset about a person suffering affliction and prays to the Holy Spirit, the response she receives reflects the apocryphal *Acts of Peter* in its description of God according to the different family roles: "I am your father in creation; I am your mother in redemption; I am your brother in divisions; I am you sister in sweet society."

[Source: Mechtild von Hackeborn *Liber Specialis Gratiae*, vol. 11 of *Revelationes Gertrudiannae et Mechtildianae*, ed. Dom Ludwig Paquelin (Paris: H. Oudin, 1877) p. 304, translated from Latin by Rev. Michael Pollitt]

In another conversation, Christ speaks to Mechtild and reveals to her that God's love is her mother and Christ is like the nursing mother who gives her child all the nourishment necessary for life and growth: "My love will be your mother, and as children suckle their mothers so you suckle from her inner consolation, indescribable sweetness, and she will feed your belly and give you drink and clothe you with everything necessary just as a mother will take care of her only daughter." [Source: Mechtild von Hackeborn *Liber Specialis Gratiae*, vol. 11 of *Revelationes Gertrudiannae et Mechtildiannae,* ed. Dom Ludwig Paquelin (Paris: H. Oudin, 1877), p. 150, translated from Latin by Rev. Michael Pollitt]

Mechtild provides still another maternal reference when she compares Christ to a mother who protects her child from danger even to the extent that she will save it from the wolf's jaws: ". . . but just as I, a mother myself of a child, meet them that I may rescue them from the jaws of wolves." (Source: Mechtild von Hackeborn, *Ibid.*, p. 53, translated by Rev. Michael Pollitt)

Mother God

"My love will be your mother, and as children suckle their mothers so you suckle from her inner consolation, indescribable sweetness, and she will feed your belly and give you drink and clothe you with everything necessary just as a mother will take care of her only daughter."

[Source: Mechtild von Hackeborn *Liber Specialis Gratiae*, vol. 11 of *Revelationes Gertrudiannae et Mechtildiannae*, ed. Dom Ludwig Paquelin (Paris: H. Oudin, 1877), p. 150, translated from Latin by Rev. Michael Pollitt]

Questions for Personal Reflection or Group Discussion

1. Did you ever experience motherly love in your life? If so, how did you feel about this experience?

2. Is it important to use maternal imagery for God in prayer and worship today? Why? Why not?

3. How can relating to God as mother provide an alternative for those who cannot relate to God as father?

4. How can relating to God as mother be a source of healing for those who have had difficulty in their relationship with their mother?

Prayer Suggestions

1. Begin by breathing deeply through your abdomen for several minutes. As you inhale slowly, be aware of God's motherly presence embracing you. As you exhale slowly, let go of all tensions, stresses, anxieties, distractions, etc.

2. Use your imagination to remember any experience you have had of motherly love in your life. As these memories come forward, be aware of your feelings. Open yourself fully to the love and power of these special times. Offer thanks to Mother God for these memories.

3. If our relationship with our mother is negative, or if we have had less than adequate mothering, the Mother God image can bring up anxiety, anger or fear. If this is so, we can experience healing within by imaging Mother God as the ideal mother who embraces us with unconditional love and affirmation. Begin by imaging yourself being held in Mother God's loving embrace. Picture

Mother God healing the difference between the love you needed and the love you received. Open yourself to Mother God as she soothes away the pain, fear, resentments of the past. Rest in Her healing love for you. Praying to Mother God can also be beneficial for those who have had difficulty relating to God as father.

4. Draw an image or mandala of Mother God. Begin by reflecting on your experiences of God's motherly love. Then draw your image or mandala.

5. Dialogue with the image or mandala you have created. Write down words, phrases describing your encounter with Mother God.

6. Our church needs to integrate feminine images into its communal prayer in order to contemplate the divine mystery more fully. Reflect on ways you can do this now by using feminine images in small faith communities. Perhaps, you could introduce feminine images in your local liturgies or in some special communal prayer celebrations. If you were able to do this, what difference would it make? Would the Christian community be enriched?

7. Invite Mother God to mother you in new ways in your life now.

8. Pray your own or any of the following mantras which express Mother God's love for you:

"I will always love you."
"You are beautiful."
"You are my beloved daughter/ son."
"You are created in my image."

9. Record your feelings, images, thoughts, insights, decisions in a journal, poetry, art, song, dance or in some other creative way.

Hildegard of Bingen

The most important female theologian of the twelfth century, Hildegard of Bingen, does not portray Christ as mother but rather uses feminine imagery to refer to the Spirit, the work of the Trinity and to describe wisdom. (Caroline Walker Bynum *Jesus as Mother*, Berkeley: University of California Press, 1982 pp. 141-142.) In Hildegard's visions, Christ's coming in the flesh is symbolized by radiant feminine figures: *Sapientia, Caritas, Ecclesia* inspired by Wisdom, *Sophia*, in the Hebrew Scriptures. In these theophanies, the feminine form still signifies the humanity of God, but now as: "the mystery hidden from ages past in God who created all things, so that the manifold wisdom of God might now be made known . . . as a plan for the fullness of times . . ." (Eph 3:9, 1:10 *NAB*). Such visionary figures portray the Word incarnate according to scholar Barbara Newman, "not as an historical fact, but as the eternal plan of God's loving providence." The visions reveal God's mercy, goodness, gentleness and tenderness. In Hildegard's first vision of the feminine Divine, she describes a radiant woman adored by angels. A voice from heaven called her *Scientia Dei*, the Knowledge of God: "She is awesome in terror as the Thunderer's lightning, and gentle in goodness as the sunshine. In her terror and her gentleness she is incomprehensible to us, because of the dread radiance of divinity in her face and the brightness which dwells in her as the robe of glory . . . For she is with all and in all, and of beauty so great in her mystery that none could comprehend how sweetly she bears with us, and how she spares us with inscrutable mercy."

[Hildegard of Bingen, *Scivias* III. 4.15; quoted in Adelgundis Fuhrkotter, *Das Leben der bl. Hildegard von Bingen* (Dusseldorf, 1968) p. 401., [Barbara Newman, "Divine Power Made Perfect in Weakness," *Peaceweavers,* edited by John A. Nicols and Lillian Thomas Shank, Kalamazoo, Michigan: Cistercian Publications, Inc.]

A Vision of the Feminine Divine

She is awesome in terror as the Thunderer's lightning, and gentle in goodness as the sunshine. In her terror and her gentleness she is incomprehensible to us, because of the dread radiance of divinity in her face and the brightness which dwells in her as the robe of glory . . . For she is with all and in all, and of beauty so great in her mystery that none could comprehend how sweetly she bears with us, and how she spares us with inscrutable mercy.

[Hildegard of Bingen, *Scivias* III.4.15; quoted in Adelgundis Fuhrkotter, *Das Leben der bl. Hildegard von Bingen* (Dusseldorf, 1968) p. 401., Barbara Newman, "Divine Power Made Perfect in Weakness," *Peaceweavers*, edited by John A. Nicols and Lillian Thomas Shank, Kalamazoo, Michigan: Cistercian Publications, Inc. (1987, pp. 113-114.)

Questions for Personal Reflection or Group Discussion

1. In Hildegard's first vision of the Feminine Divine she saw a brilliant woman adored by angels. A voice from heaven identified her as the Knowledge of God. What images come to mind when you encounter the Feminine Divine as the Knowledge of God in Hildegard's vision?

2. How do you feel about these images?

3. What impact do you think women's understandings and insights have on society? the church? the world?

4. What do you think the Feminine Divine wants to communicate with us through the contemporary awareness of women's experiences and consciousness?

Prayer Suggestions

1. With your eyes closed and your body relaxed, journey to your still point where the Feminine Divine dwells. Spend some time simply being present to the Feminine Divine.

2. Contemplate Hildegard's vision. Immerse yourself in the Feminine Divine's knowledge, beauty, terror, gentleness, and mercy.

3. Reflect upon the times you have experienced being known by God in your life in the past. Be aware of what you have learned from these times about yourself, others, and God.

4. Look for signs of new life, growth, hope, change, renewal in your life now. Make a list of these situations or relationships. Be conscious of what the Feminine Divine is revealing to you through these signs. What does the Feminine Divine reveal to you that is difficult? challenging? frightening? wonderful? joyful? Be open to any new insights or understandings you may receive from Her.

5. Reflect on your vision for the future. Who are you? Who do you want to be? What do you value? What role might the Feminine Divine play in the unfolding of your vision? How do you feel about your growing consciousness of the Feminine Divine? How does this knowledge differ from your earlier understanding of God? Write down your response to these questions.

6. Reflect upon insights, understandings, values that come from women's experiences that are enriching and changing politics, culture, business practices, women's roles, religion etc. You might want to conduct a dialogue asking the Feminine Divine to reveal to you Her role as a change agent in the empowerment of women in one of these areas.

7. Light a candle and allow it to serve as a symbol of the empowerment of women by the Feminine Divine. Contemplate this great mystery of grace. Pray with expectant hope for women you know who need to be empowered. Pray for the empowerment of all women everywhere especially in cultures in which women are the most oppressed from cradle to grave.

8. Celebrate women's empowerment with friends, companions or community by some ritual in a small group setting. (One of many approaches: begin with music, do a reflective exercise from this book, share a symbol of the Feminine Divine, express the power of this symbol through art, poetry, pottery, needlepoint, song, dance, mime or in some other creative way the group chooses.

9. Do something to raise consciousness about women's issues. (sexual violence and abuse, harassment, unjust hiring practices, reproduction issues, treatment of women as less than human in some cultures etc.) One suggestion is to join a group that lobbies for women's rights. Another possibility, if you are a woman, is to join a women's support group. Record your feelings, images, thoughts, insights, decisions in a journal, poetry, art, song, dance or in some other creative way.

Marguerite of Oingt

In thirteenth and fourteenth century medieval mystics' writings, female imagery changes from nursing with milk to nursing with blood. For example, Lutgard of Aywieres (1246) describes visions of Christ dying on the cross in which she nurses from his breast, drinking in consolation and comfort with the blood: "Do not wean me, good Jesus, from the breast of thy consolation . . . there is safety for me in hastening to thy embrace." [Source: The monk of Farne, "Meditations," Chaps. 40 and 50-51 ed. Farmer, pp. 182-183 and 189-90 trans. a Benedictine nun of Stanbrook, *The Monk of Farne: Meditations of a Fourteenth-Century Monk,* ed. Hugh Farmer, The Benedictine Studies (Baltimore, 1961),pp. 64 and 73-74.] Laboring in great pain to give birth is emphasized along with suckling and union with Mother Jesus. The Carthusian prioress Marguerite of Oingt (d.1310) who did not wish to have any father or mother except God compares Christ's life and death to a mother's labor for her baby's birth. In her work, *Pagina Meditationum*, Maguerite asks Christ if he is not her mother more than her mother since her mother labored to give her birth a single day or night, but Christ labored to give her spiritual life for more than thirty years. "Nor do I have father or mother besides you nor do I wish to have. For are you not my mother and more than my mother? The mother who bore me labored in delivering me for one day or one night but you, my sweet and lovely Lord, labored for me for more than thirty years." Marguerite compares the drops of blood from the cross to the sweat of giving birth: "But when the time approached for you to be delivered, your labor pains were so great that your holy sweat was like great drops of blood that came out from your body and fell on the earth." Marguerite extends this analogy further by comparing Christ's cross to the bed of labor and by describing the rupture of Christ's veins that occurred in giving birth to the world in a single day. (Source: Marguerite d'Oingt, *Pagina Meditationum*, Chaps. 30-39, *Oeuvres*, pp. 77-79 quoted in Bynum, *Jesus as Mother*, pp. 152-153)

Mother Jesus Birthing the World

For you not my mother and more than my mother? The mother who bore me labored in delivering me for one day or one night but you, my sweet and lovely Lord, labored for me for more than thirty years. Ah, my sweet and lovely Lord, with what love you labored for me and bore me through your whole life. But when the time approached for you to be delivered, your labor pains were so great that your holy sweat was like great drops of blood that came out from your body and fell on the earth . . . Ah! Sweet Lord Jesus Christ, who ever saw a mother suffer such a birth! For when the hour of your delivery came you were placed on the hard bed of the cross . . . and your nerves and all your veins were broken. And truly it is no surprise that your veins burst when in one day you gave birth to the whole world. (Marguerite of Oingt (1310), *Pagina,* chaps. 30-39, *Oeuvres,* pp. 77-79. quoted in Caroline Walker Bynum, *Jesus as Mother*, Berkeley: University of California Press, 1982, p. 153)

Questions for Personal Reflection or Group Discussion

1. Have you given birth to a baby? If so, what effect did this experience have on you?

2. Have you ever felt like you gave birth to yourself? How did this feel?

3. Have you ever felt like you gave birth to another person spiritually?

4. How does Christ continue to give birth to the world today through people? through the church? through you?

Prayer Suggestions

1. Allow your body to relax . . . Feel your head and neck relax . . . Relax your eyes, nose, and mouth . . . Let go of any tensions in the back of your neck, shoulders and back . . . Feel your arms and hands relax . . . Your chest, abdomen, and hips are relaxing . . . Relax your legs, knees, feet. Do this exercise for several minutes or as long as it takes to relax.

2. As you read Marguerite's reflection, let the maternal imagery of Jesus on the cross giving birth to the world speak to you. Are you comfortable with this imagery? Why? Why not?

3. Have you given birth to a baby? Reflect on the suffering you felt during labor and childbirth. Remember how it felt to nurture your infant at the breast. Be aware of those intimate moments of bonding with your newborn. How did you express maternal love for your baby? Recall these times and thank God for the gift of motherhood. Be aware specifically, of ways your experience of giving birth helped you to grow spiritually.

4. Recall a time when you labored to bring forth new life in some area of your life. Remember the pain and struggle you endured. Pay attention to any thoughts, feelings, images, insights that emerge as you reflect on this experience. Be aware of ways that you grew spiritually at this time.

5. Choose a symbol of this experience. Place this symbol in a significant place as a reminder of your birthing experience. As you contemplate this symbol, be aware of how divine grace is birthing you anew in different situations and relationships each day.

6. Reflect on a time in your life when you struggled to give birth to another person spiritually. How did you feel? What happened? Conduct a dialogue with this person about this experience. What, if anything, would you do differently if you had this opportunity today?

7. Image Christ giving birth to the world today through the suffering and labor of ordinary people . . . political, religious, spiritual leaders . . . the poor and oppressed. . . . you . . . etc. Reflect on something you could do to actively participate in the process of giving birth to the new creation. Be conscious of different groups and communities who commit themselves to work for a better world (environmental protection, human rights, justice, peace and equality etc.). Be aware of any thoughts, feelings, images, insights, sensations that emerge.

8. Make a list of these or draw a world and fill it with words and images that describe your response to #7. Ask for the strength you need to work with others in our world and/or church to birth the new creation.

9. Record your feelings, images, thoughts, insights, decisions in a journal, poetry, art, song, dance or in some other creative way.

Julian of Norwich

The fourteenth-century English anchoress and mystic, Julian of
Norwich in her *Revelations of Divine Love* develops a rich, innovative theology of the motherhood of God. For Julian, there is no
human relationship capable of portraying the love of God better
than feminine motherly love. Her *Revelations* contain four chap-
ters (58-61) devoted to the development of the divine maternal
image. Julian uses the word "mother" or some variation of this
word eighty-three times throughout the Revelations. The majority
of these references associate the title with God. Over thirty of
these references explicitly refer to Jesus Christ, the second person
of the Trinity. "To Julian, God is never simply like a mother,"
observes Jennifer Perone Heimmel, (God) . . . "is a mother and the
most ultimate of mothers." (Source: Heimmel, p. 60.)

Julian's portrayal of God as a human mother encompasses a
rich diversity of images ranging from the images of nursing
Mother God found in the biblical, patristic and mystical writers,
to the more obscure images of God the Mother who feeds the child
with the sacrament of the Eucharist found in Clement of Alexandria and John Chrysostom. Julian writes: "The mother can give
her child a suck of milk, but our precious mother Jesus feeds us
with himself and does most courteously and most tenderly, with
the blessed sacrament . . ." (Trans. Edmund Colledge and James
Walsh, *Julian of Norwich: Showings* Classics of Western Spirituality, New York: Paulist Press, 1978, Chapter 60, p. 298.) Like
Augustine of Hippo, Thomas Aquinas, Albert the Great, Julian
also identifies the wisdom of God as our mother: "And the deep
wisdom of the Trinity is our mother, in whom we are enclosed."
(*Showings*, chapter 54, p. 285.) Like the apocryphal *Acts of Peter,*
Mechtild von Hackeborn, Julian includes God as mother among a
list of other family roles: "And so I saw that God rejoices that he
is our Father, and God rejoices that he is our Mother, and God
rejoices that he is our true spouse . . ." (*Showings*, chapter 52, p.
279.) Also, Julian, like Albert the Great, the Monk of Farne, and
Marguerite of Oingt believes that God is more a mother than our
human mother: "And though our earthly mother may suffer her
child to perish, our heavenly Mother Jesus may never suffer us
who are his children to perish, for he is almighty, all wisdom and
all love, and so is none but he, blessed may he be." (*Showings*,
chapter 61, p. 301) Unlike Maguerite of Oingt, Julian's love for
Mother God, does not result in a rejection of the earthly mother

but instead expresses affirmation for the earthly mother's role in creation. According to Julian, God is the perfect mother who loves us totally, passionately and unconditionally from conception until death.[2]

OUR
PRECIOUS
MOTHER JESUS
FEEDS US
WITH HIMSELF

---

2. See Heimmel's dissertation for an in-depth exploration of the Motherhood of God in Julian Norwich, pp. 57-83.

The Wisdom of the Trinity as our Mother

Julian of Norwich

"As to the first, I saw and understood that the high might of the Trinity is our Father, and the deep wisdom of the Trinity is our Mother, and the great love of the Trinity is our Lord; and all these we have in nature and in our substantial creation . . .

"Thus in our Father, God almighty, we have our being, and in our Mother of mercy we have our reforming and our restoring, in whom our parts are united and all made perfect . . . and through the rewards and gifts of grace of the Holy Spirit we are fulfilled. And our substance is in our Father, God almighty, and our substance is in our Mother , God all wisdom, and our substance is in our Lord God, the Holy Spirit, all goodness, for our substance is whole in each person of the Trinity, who is one God." (Source: Trans. Edmund Colledge and James Walsh. *Julian of Norwich: Showings* Classics of Western Spirituality, New York: Paulist Press, 1978, Chapter 58, pp. 294-295)

Questions for Personal Reflection or Group Discussion

1. From this passage and your reflection on it, what new images or understandings of the Trinity as our Mother did you experience?

2. In what ways does the Trinity "mother" us?

3. How have you experienced the Wisdom of the Trinity as "Mother" in your life?

4. In what ways can you be a reflection of the Wisdom of the Trinity in the world? How is the Trinity a reflection of God's mothering presence in the world?

Prayer Suggestions

1. Close your eyes. Relax your body. Spend several minutes in silence delighting in the Trinity's "mothering" activity in your life and in the world.

2. Let your imagination explore the fullness of these images of "God our Mother . . . who is wisdom . . . reforming . . . restoring" . . . your inmost being, . . . "in whom our parts are united and all made perfect." Be aware of any thoughts, feelings, images, insights, sensations that emerge.

3. Reflect on the mystery of the Trinity. Write down any new names, metaphors, symbols, relationships, understandings or intuitions that come to you. Draw a mandala or image of your "picture" of the Trinity if you wish.

4. Imagine yourself in the presence of the Trinity. Open yourself to the "mothering" activity of God. Be aware of any feelings, new insights into God as Mother that come to you.

5. Listen to the Wisdom of the Trinity as She reveals Her "mothering" activity in your life.

6. Become aware of yourself as a unique reflection of the Wisdom of the Trinity in the world. How has being a woman or man shaped your understanding of the Trinity? What impact does your "wise mothering" have on others? on the suffering and poor in the world? etc.

7. Ask Mother God to reveal to you ways in which you can reflect Her wisdom in your life-style, relationships, work, play etc.

8. Decide on one thing you will do to celebrate the Wisdom of the Trinity as your Mother. (Join in the cosmic dance of the universe, create a symbol in art or clay that reflects this mystery, compose music etc.)

9. Record your feelings, images, thoughts, insights, decisions in a journal, poetry, art, song, dance or in some other creative way.

Merciful Mother Jesus

Julian of Norwich

"For we shall truly see in heaven without end that we have sinned grievously in this life . . . And by the experience of this falling we shall have a great and marvelous knowledge of love in God without end; for enduring and marvelous is that love which cannot and will not be broken because of offenses . . .

"The mother may sometimes suffer the child to fall and to be distressed in various ways, for its own benefit, but she can never suffer any kind of peril to come to her child because of her love. And though our earthly mother may suffer her child to perish, our heavenly Mother Jesus may never suffer us . . . to perish.

"But often when our falling and our wretchedness are shown to us, we are so much afraid and so greatly ashamed of ourselves that we scarcely know where we can put ourselves. But then our courteous Mother does not wish us to flee away . . . but . . . to behave like a child. For when it is distressed and frightened, it runs quickly to its mother; and if it can do no more, it calls to the mother for help with all its might . . . "My gracious Mother, my beloved Mother have mercy on me." (Source: Trans. Edmund Colledge and James Walsh. *Julian of Norwich: Showings* Classics of Western Spirituality, New York: Paulist Press, 1978, Chapter 61, pp. 300-301)

Questions for Personal Reflection or Group Discussion

1. How did you experience your own mother?

2. Do you need healing in your relationship with your mother?

3. Have there been times that you experienced the merciful love of Mother Jesus in your life?

4. In what ways do you reflect the merciful love of Mother Jesus to others?

Prayer Suggestions

1. Begin this prayer experience by reciting one of these mantras or by creating your own prayer phrase.

"Merciful Mother heal me."

"Mother Jesus free me."

"Mother Jesus love me."

"Mother Jesus have mercy."

2. Recall your mother. Offer thanks for the ways she "mothered" you. Offer her forgiveness for any hurt, deprivation, abuse, that you experienced in your relationship with her. Ask her to forgive you for anything you may have done or failed to do that hurt her. You may wish to write a letter to your mother expressing your love and gratitude to her for being your mother. If it is appropriate, ask for forgiveness and offer forgiveness.

3. Read Julian's passage. Then close your eyes and let your imagination experience Mother Jesus. Ask your divine Mother to embrace you in the area of your greatest needs and deepest fears.

4. Invite Mother Jesus to heal any wounds that remain in your relationship with your mother.

5. Be aware of any thoughts, feelings, images that emerge, as you pray for healing in this relationship. Share these with Mother Jesus.

6. Offer thanks for any healing that occurred in your relationship with your mother during this prayer experience.

7. Celebrate this healing by doing something loving for your mother. If your mother is deceased, do something loving for someone who needs mothering in their life.

8. Look at today's newspaper. Notice the articles that show suffering, violence, hostility etc. Pray for those who need mercy in our world. Then in the same newspaper, find articles that show people being merciful to others. Offer thanks for them. Be aware of how you can be a reflection of the merciful love of Mother Jesus to others.

9. Record your feelings, images, thoughts, insights, decisions in a journal, poetry, art, song, dance or in some other creative way.

Part Four

Reflections of Contemporary Women

Today women and men are expanding their images of God to include the feminine. Women are affirming their identity as women, created in *imago Dei*, as one with the feminine of God. Men are celebrating their identity as men, while at the same time embracing their feminine side without fear. Both women and men are finding that praying with feminine images of God is a liberating, healing experience which fosters greater balance, wholeness and freedom in their lives. Using female imagery to describe our experience of God leads us to a larger vision of and a greater appreciation of divine activity. Indeed, praying with feminine images of God not only liberates us but also liberates God from a masculine-only representation and domination!

In the following guided prayer experiences contemporary women from different backgrounds draw us gently into powerful meditative encounters with the Feminine Divine in our midst. Each reflection, discussion question and prayer suggestion is a gift which comes from the inner journey of each woman's spirit self. As the stories, metaphors and prayers of each woman are shared, we are invited to journey with the Feminine Divine who will heal, free and transform the way we see ourselves, each other, and the world. Let us delight together in the Feminine Divine!

Ammah's Lullaby

We may think of God as "*Abba*" (Daddy); but in the same vein, we may focus on the feminine dimension, calling God "*Ammah*"" (Mommy). Bonaventure speaks of all humankind being conceived in the womb of eternal wisdom, who "later, gave birth by suffering in the flesh." (See *Exploring the Feminine Face of God*, p. 47) *Ammah's* lullaby speaks to each of us caught up in her unbounded, unconditional and efficacious love.

I wombed you,
I bloomed you,
    I nourished your forming.
I birthed you
And earthed you
    And bled for your coming.
I nurtured you,
Searched for you
    through childish roamings;
Believed in
Your daylights and
    Grieved through your gloamings.

I buried a potency
    A trust in your holding;
I spun the genetic chain
    Guides your unfolding.

I know that I loved you
    Before your first sun,
And continue enfolding
    that all may forth come!

(Regina Madonna Oliver, S.S.C., M.A., M.T.S., Pastoral Associate at Fort Belvoir Chapel, Alexandria, Virginia)

Questions for Personal Reflection or Discussion

1. If you have experienced calling our God-Source "*Abba*" (Daddy, Dad) as Jesus did, can you find comfort in calling God "*Ammah*" (Mama, Mom), when you think of the nurturing, mothering way God interacts in your life?

2. Think of your own relationship with your father/your mother. Sometimes negative memories about out human relationships can affect our using these human metaphors in thinking of God. How

do your parent recollections affect your thinking of God as "Mama?"

3. How much of the "potency" hidden within you have you been able to develop into positive character traits and gifts? Have you considered that your mothering God created you with amazing potential? What would you like to develop next in the area of your giftedness?

4. Have you considered your Mothering God as one who loves you into existence; as one who never gives up on you; who is determined to bring you to integration and maturity? How does this idea affect you?

Prayer Suggestions

1. Reflect backward through your years. *At each stopping point where your reflection seems to stand still for a moment pray: "Oh, Ammah, my God and my Source, heal the hurts that come from the difference between the love I needed and the love I received."* Move from the present, back and back, to the time when you were an infant, totally dependent, nursing at the breast, or crying for your mother's arms. Sink further backward to the time of your nine months of formation in the womb. Then move back to the moment of your conception. Sink beyond this, and slip into the mind of God, your Mother-Source, who sees the wholeness of you in the grasp of an eternal now. *Ammah* wills you into being, into growth, into fulfillment. Rest in the comfort of this realization.

2. Read the poem *"Ammah's* Lullaby" again. *Ammah* is speaking this to you, more surely, more securely than any earthly mother can. This is because there are aspects of your being which only your God-Source can know thoroughly or touch and heal gently- such as your "genetic chain," your inherited tendencies, your hidden potential. Neither your birth-mother nor yourself have a grasp of these innermost workings of your being.

3. Rest in the overpowering reality of *Ammah's* penetrating love. She knows the whole of you and says "yes!" to your existence.

4. Let sweet waves of awareness of being so intimately known and loved flow over you as long as their tide keeps inflowing. Respond in love and thanks to *Ammah*.

5. There is bleeding in childbirth; we all know that. The bleeding death of Jesus as giver and promise of our new life, our godly life, although it is shadowed in mystery, is easily accessible to our symbol sense. Jesus' redemptive action is an indication of the pre-

ciousness of this godly new-life of ours to *Ammah*, our Mother-Source.

6. Read the poem again from the line "I nurtured you," slowly, with the following in mind. We have heard time and again that God's love for us is "unconditional"—not influenced by our *faux-pas*—nor even by our total reversals. This Unconditional Love believes in our becoming all we can be, and never gives up in its inner movement to bring about our triumphant denouement.

7. Think of the potential you find in yourself. Some of this "potency" you have developed. Be happy for that and don't be afraid to name these successes. Since you have not reached your terminus, there is still "potency" left to unfold or be developed. Some of this you know and can name. Do so now in the presence of *Ammah*, with a grateful heart. Some of your undeveloped potential you suspect, as a secret desire, a tantalizing challenge. Let these name themselves for you with *Ammah's* help. Tell *Ammah* which you will seek to develop next.

8. Enter into conversation with *Ammah* about your integration, your maturing process—the unfolding of your gifts. Reflect that all giftedness is given that it may be forth-given for the benefit of others, who are also loved and gifted by *Ammah*. Tell *Ammah* you wish to be open to being all that She creates you to be.

9. Creatively resolve your prayer time by writing a thank you to *Ammah* in your journal, bursting into poetry or song, sketching, or responding in another art form of your choice.

Grandmother God

I think of my own grandmother who was very dear to me . . . the one who enriched my life . . . taught me the meaning of love . . . and of how much my Grandmother reflects the God who loves me . . .

If I listen closely and concentrate I can hear Grandmother God as She faces with me the obstacles in my path. She questions; as she compassionates my weakness, asking herself:

Can I help my child? . . .

Is she afraid? . . .

Why is she sad? . . .

What makes my child cry? . . .

Does my little one need me? . . .

What makes her worry? . . .

Does she miss me? . . .

God our Grandmother has a special closeness to us that is affirmed by an overwhelming consuming endearment . . . one we share with our own grandmother . . . the one who taught us how to pray . . . who opened our hearts to a God of mercy, a God of love.

My thoughts also dwell on my own granddaughter . . . the joy of my life . . . the one whom I am teaching how to pray . . . the one with whom I want to share my "Grandmother God's" love, a devotional love; that she, too, will someday share with her own granddaughter.

My Grandmother God the jewel of my existence. I am precious to Her. I try to please Her. She resides in me and I am one in her. In Her life-giving presence I dwell in gleeful exultation.

My oneness with God my Grandmother is a linkage to the strong women of the Exodus who first experienced the loving, caring, sharing of a Grandmother God who reached out to them . . . placed them in Her protective care . . . and guided them in their journey . . . just as She guides us, Her grandchildren, on our pilgrimage through life.

My Grandmother God has shared with me some wonderful secrets and awesome surprises that make being a grandmother a never-ending delight and challenge!

(Bettie McNamara Fretz M.A., Grandmother, Writer, Public Relations/Management Consultant; former Washington correspondent and syndicated columnist.)

Questions for Personal Reflection or Group Discussion

1. What is my relationship with God my Grandmother? Are we friends? Do we have differences to resolve?

2. What has grandmother-love taught you about being, literally the "apple of one's eye"? Are you not the "apple of God's eye"?

3. In what way(s) do you think people experience a spiritual yearning for Grandmother-God's provident care today?

4. Grandmothers have a special privilege. They may spoil their grandchildren a bit. Does Grandmother God spoil you?

Prayer Suggestions

1. Turn your thoughts within. Think of the times you have been close to God your Grandmother. Think of all the scattered fragmented periods of your life when all seemed lost but She was there with you.

2. As you reflect on your own grandmother or on your relationship with a granddaughter, visualize the image of God your Grandmother. Write a letter to Grandmother God. Summarize what your thoughts about your own Grandmothers' experiences have helped you understand about the uniqueness of God's love for you or recalling stories of your grandmothers, and great grandmothers, symbolize your family heritage in drawing, poetry, song, or in some other artistic expression.

3. Feel the warmth of Grandmother God's compassion . . . know that she will always love you. Share your needs with Her now.

4. Listen to Her response to your needs. Then spend a few moments in stillness reflecting on your relationship with Grandmother God.

5. Try to picture the grandmothers of your past generations. Some were poor . . . some had comfortable lives, but their greatest richness was the faith they passed on to their descendants. Contemplate the depths of their love for Grandmother God.

6. Visualize the trials and tragedies in each of their life spans . . . birth, death, war, famine, the loss of home, country. etc. Dwell on the courage with which they faced pulling up stakes, immigration, leaving loved ones. etc. Take note of their strength

and the wisdom of Grandmother God who accompanied them every step of the way.

7. Create a litany of the grandmothers whose names you know, as well as those whose identity is lost in oblivion. God our grandmother who loves us knew and lead each of them. She suffered with them . . . shared their joys and sorrows. Each of them passed on to us their ardent love for God.

8. Now close your mind to the sounds surrounding you and listen to Her voice within you. Touch the face of Grandmother God, feel Her nearness to you. Rest in Her love for you.

9. Record your feelings, images, thoughts, insights, decisions in a journal, poetry, art, song, dance or in some other creative way.

Delighting in the Magic of the Feminine Divine

We can all remember stories we read as children in which a magic person appeared to save the hero or heroine from fate. Often portrayed as a fairy, magician, godmother queen, or good witch the magic person performed outstanding deeds which facilitated the arrival for the main character.

As children we believed in a magic person. As we grew, became more rational and scientific (even perhaps a bit dull), and prided ourselves on how sophisticated we were, we outgrew our belief in magic. Magic, in general, took a bad rap.

The object of magic, however, is to make what is hidden known. The magic person in our fairy tales never had to do more than read the heart of the main character and set a process in motion by which the journey person came to know the truth.

To delight in the magic of the Feminine Divine is to trust that we can know our own truth, that our hearts can be read and understood by others, that process is vastly more important than product, and that we live in a magic world full of ambiguity, miracles, symbols of divine presence, and delight.

The magic of the Feminine Divine speaks when flowers manage to push through frozen earth each spring, when a friend asks us questions which challenge our preconceived notions, when a poet speaks to our hearts, when each day and each night the sun and moon reveal their light, and when we gaze upon our children knowing they came through us.

The Feminine Divine is full of magic powers given to us in the forms of creation, compassion, consciousness, hope, journey, and love. To delight in these gifts means we view ourselves as magic people for each other, read each others' hearts, delighting in truth, stroking that which is wounded in order to heal, celebrating the festivals of life.

To be a magic person means to believe what is unknown can be explored, experienced, and made known to us through the divine presence. To be magic means to be co-creator with divinity and thus leave as our legacy the belief that indeed, all things are possible.

Whether we name divine presence "synchronicity," "serendipity," or "graced moment" matters little. What matters is the reality that our hearts have been understood. Nothing is as real as a healthy dose of magic which restores our spirits. The Feminine Divine delights in the festivals of magic and sets in motion the process by which we come to know our own truth. That it is possible to reflect on who we are in relation to earth, each other, and the divine is the nature of magic, blessed and given that we might have life.

(Nancy Long M.A., M.S.)

Questions for Personal Reflection or Group Discussion

1. Recall a favorite story from childhood which contains a magic person. Why do you remember the story? How does it continue to inform your life?

2. What did the magic person communicate to the main character in the story?

3. What did the main character need to learn about himself/herself?

4. Who has been a magic person in your own life? Name that person and name what her/she helped you know about yourself?

Prayer Suggestions

1. Create a prayer focal point around some magic symbols, e.g. flowers, candles, books, thread, photographs etc. Assume a comfortable position by the focal point and relax, concentrate on your breathing until you can center your thoughts on what the symbols offer to you.

2. Close your eyes and image the Feminine Divine in a way which visualizes your concept of a magic person.

3. Ask the image the ways in which magic occurs around you which you are unable to see. Listen to the answer.

4. Give your blessing to that image, thanking Her for Her gifts to you.

5. Think of the ways you have been magic for other people. Visualize these people. Ask them what they would have you know more fully about yourself.

6. Visualize your own bedroom. What symbols do you have there which are magic?

7. Who gave you the most magic symbols you have? Think of those persons. Thank them for their gifts to you.

8. Lift your heart up to your divine sacred presence. Image your body becoming magic. What can you do with your magic body? To whom can you bring a gift?

9. Stop your prayer by returning to focus on your breathing. When finished, celebrate your prayer in a way suitable to your expression. Plant a flower, record your experience in a journal, draw the image you saw, kiss your child, and take time to play.

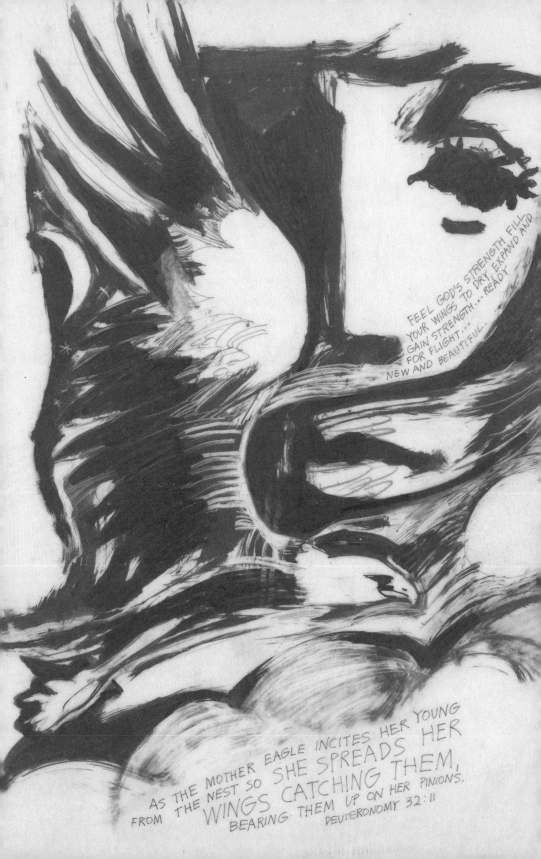

FEEL GOD'S STRENGTH FILL
YOUR WINGS TO DRY EXPAND AND
GAIN STRENGTH... READY
FOR FLIGHT...
NEW AND BEAUTIFUL.

AS THE MOTHER EAGLE INCITES HER YOUNG
FROM THE NEST SO SHE SPREADS HER
WINGS CATCHING THEM,
BEARING THEM UP ON HER PINIONS.
DEUTERONOMY 32:11

Mother Eagle and the Reluctant Risk-Taker

"As the mother eagle incites her young from the nest" (it is sometimes her way to push a reluctant eaglet from the cliff to teach it to fly) "so she spread her wings catching them, bearing them up on her pinions." (Deuteronomy 32:11, *NRSV*)

(Nanette M. Wisser MSC, M.A.)

Questions for Personal Reflection or Group Discussion

1. What are the secure "nests" to which you cling?

2. What risk(s) are you being called to take?

3. Why do you find surrendering security so difficult?

4. What are your fears? losses? Can you look for and admit them?

Prayer Suggestions

1. Be aware of your breathing as you breathe in strength and courage. Breathe out weaknesses, fears etc.

2. Present your fears, struggles to your tender Mother God hovering over you.

3. Listen as She urges you to risk . . . to leave the cliff to fly . . . Feel the strength of Her wings hovering over you.

4. Be aware of the "falling" which risk entails . . . yet Mother Eagle is always near . . . tenderly urging . . . gently prodding . . . reassuring with the strength of Her strong wings.

5. You can no longer resist . . . her prodding has you over the cliff . . . You flutter, fly, falter . . . With a squeal for help . . . you fall . . . onto the outstretched wings of Mother Eagle.

6. You rest, frightened yet trusting, as mother eagle carries you back to the cliff . . . settles you on the edge . . . and again urges, prods you to risk.

7. Reflect on any insights, strengths, new feelings of courage that came to you during this time of prayer.

8. Share with Mother God any risks you now feel ready to take.

9. Record your feelings, images, thoughts, insights, decisions in a journal, poetry, art, song, dance or in some other creative way.

Mother God—Maker of the Beautiful

To become a butterfly the caterpillar hangs in an awkward position on a fragile web as the life's fluid drips from its body. At the same time a death-like chrysalis is forming.

When the chrysalis is complete, it hangs as if dead until it is transformed. Inside, the caterpillar turns to liquid.

When the butterfly is completely patterned, it burst out—emerges, wet, ugly and uncertain. Then it waits—the butterfly waits until faith in its wings is strong enough. At the right moment, the butterfly takes off never to return to the broken chrysalis.

(Sr. Nanette M. Wisser MSC, M.A.)

Questions for Personal Reflection or Group Discussion

1. What are some things in your life that need to be transformed?

2. What is necessary to bring about transformation?

3. Why is surrender so difficult? Can transformation take place without surrender?

4. In what ways have you experienced Mother God as Maker of the Beautiful in your life? in your relationships? in your communities? in the world?

Prayer Suggestions

1. Be aware of your breathing.

   Breathe in . . . "Mother strengthen me."
   Breathe out . . . "I surrender in trust."

2. Sense your helplessness as you hang . . . the chrysalis is forming around you.

3. Imagine your being, little by little, becoming liquid . . . pure pliable liquid. Allow your tender Mother to hold you . . . to mold you . . . shaping and transforming you.

4. Bring to Her in trustfull surrender that which you want (need) Her tender love to transform . . . surrender in trust to Mother God, Maker of Beauty.

5. See yourself being patterned in greater kindness, more compassion, deeper understanding, greater desire for justice, tender warmth toward all. See your good and your beauty coming forth.

6. Feel the cramped closeness of your new beautiful self in the now too small chrysalis . . . as you breathe in strength and trust . . . and burst the chrysalis to emerge . . . wet and unsteady.

7. Breathe in your newness as you feel God's strength fill your wings to dry, expand and gain strength . . . ready for flight . . . new and beautiful.

8. Be aware of the feelings, insights, fears that you experience as you fly from the broken chrysalis never to return . . . soaring in beauty, freedom, newness.

9. Record your feelings, images, thoughts, insights, decisions in a journal, poetry, art, song, dance or in some other creative way.

Wisdom as Playful Craftswoman

Several years ago, while reading Proverbs 8:27-31, I was struck by how natural it seemed for wisdom to be playing and delighting the Creator in the act of creation. This verse has become a great guide for me on my own path of spiritual growth. The following are questions and thoughts that were formed while sitting quietly with Wisdom: Playful Craftswoman.

Questions for Personal Reflection or Group Discussion

1. How do I make this day a happy one for myself?

(Gratitude is the way which you unlock the doors of happiness at any time. Take time throughout the day to simply observe, feel, taste, smell and hear someone or something right in front of you. Receive the gift. Appreciate it. Take it in and let it move through you. Thank whoever or whatever it is silently or overtly for giving the gift. Don't try to hold on to it. Always let go. Whatever part of the gift that is meant to remain with you, will for its appropriate time. Simply be grateful. Be grateful simply.)

2. How can I help others to play?

(Be who you are. Give full expression to your inner child who delights in the treasures of creation. Share your own laughter, humor, and natural essence freely with others. It will be more difficult for others to resist it then be touched by it for when something is true and good, the spirit acknowledges it. Laughter is contagious and can be "caught" by many for healing.)

3. How do we co-create?

(Flow with the source within you in each moment. Each moment is being created. Learn from past moments. Listen to the guidance of your own inner wisdom in the present moment to do what is necessary now to create your next moment. If you trust the love your source has for you, you will continue to move into your future moments co-creating what is best for you. When others do the same, together many moments and environments are created and formed by the source that guides us all . . . love. The love source does not impose your good on others in a way that would be harmful to them. It also knows when something is being imposed on you that would be harmful to you and guides you away from it. This is why it is important to listen and stay in the glow this guidance. Trust these waters of wisdom to take you to your highest and greatest good.)

4. What insights, feelings, thoughts, images, memories, sensations does the image of Wisdom as the "Playful Craftswoman" stir within you?

At this point all was quiet and I felt like it was a good time to take my morning shower. I guess the "waters of wisdom" prompted this. While in the shower I reflected on what I had just written. I allowed myself to enjoy the pleasure of the moment. The wonderful warm water ran all over my "hills and valleys" delighting my skin. I lathered my hair and pulled back the shower curtain so I could see the mirror. I tried out all kinds of hair designs the way I used to with my daughter when she was small. I could look like a punk rocker, Lolita, Daisy Mae, or even Mamie Eisenhower. I made the appropriate faces to go with the designs. It was fun. I was laughing and feeling good throughout my being. I enjoyed the fond memories of bath play with my daughter and was grateful for the gift. My spirit was definitely up for the start of the day.

I realized how we co-create an image of ourselves every day with the ways we choose to wear our hair, our colors and clothes, and even the faces we choose to show the public. The foods I choose to put in my body and the ways I choose to prepare and eat them are also acts of creation but are all of these acts of co-creation? I think not. Foods that are toxic to my system would not be chosen by my inner wisdom. It is when I have a peace, inner joy, and sense of wholeness that I am most aware I have been moving with more of myself than usual. That "more" is my inner source who knows what most fulfills me and allows me to give my best.

When I am playing, dancing, laughing, and creating with delight I am clearly reflecting the face of God as Wisdom: Playful Craftswoman. I am very grateful for the discovery of my own gifts of playfulness and creativity which served me well in my own process of healing after the losses of loved ones. My life and professional work is now committed to helping others discover their own.

(Donna M. Mogan, Ph.D.)

Prayer Suggestions

1. Center yourself. Hold a blob of clay and let your hands do whatever they want with it. At the end of the meditation or con-

templation look at the form. Write about it in your journal or dialogue with it.

2. Place a picture of something or someone including yourself in clear view. Put on some quiet background music. While looking at the picture begin to move your body to the thoughts and feelings that arise. Our bodies also hold our impressions of people, objects and events. If you don't believe this imagine a lemon for thirty seconds and see what your mouth does. Let your body communicate with you.

3. Dance naked to some wild music either alone or with your mate. Feel yourself breaking free of the "shoulds" and "oughts" and be invigorated.

4. Sit quietly or with soft background music listening to Wisdom: Playful Craftswoman in your heart. Have before you a large pad of paper and crayons, water colors, pastels, or colored pencils or whatever medium appeals to you. As you feel a "nudge" from within allow each hand to choose its own colors. Then let each hand freely express itself on the paper. Do this as long as it feels comfortable. Your picture may be very abstract. Stand up and move your body to whatever thoughts or feelings may arise as you look at your picture. Entitle the picture and write about it somewhere on either side of the paper.

5. Prayerfully make a collage of yourself or a loved one. Simply go through old magazines and cut out pictures, words, or phrases that seem to appeal to you. Arrange them in any form on a large piece of paper and date it. Do it again six months later.

6. Immerse yourself in water, i.e. a tub, pool, jacuzzi, lake or ocean. Watch it , feel all parts of yourself in it, taste it, smell it, listen to it. Remember where you come from. Enjoy its gift and be grateful.

7. Image God as the "Playful Craftswoman" delighting in you . . . loving you . . . singing to you . . . dancing with you . . . blessing you . . . empowering you.

8. Be aware of any images, words, feelings, insights, sensations that emerge.

9. Record your feelings, images, thoughts, insights, decisions in a journal, poetry, art, song, dance or in some other creative way.

The Fruits of God's Mother-Touch

In the mother's caress, wiping away baby tears; in the healing hands of the Sister-doctor cleansing leprous wounds on Molokai; in the unwavering strength of a maternal hand stretched out to rescue her child from a sweeping flood—in all of these can be found the Divine Motherhood of God.

In our high-tech, but highly impersonal world, the warm, enveloping embrace of the Mother-God is what we yearn for. And, on the other side of touch, we depend on the tenacious, fortitudinal strength of a maternal saving hand.

Our disconnection has made us lose sight of our connection to all beings- the Being. Like the unbelieving Peter, then, about to sink into the sea, we too cry out, "God, save me!" And the maternal hand of God, so soothing and so salvaging, is always there— our steadfast friend!

The same healing hand that restores us also reconciles us to each other. How often has our earthly mother listened to our childish woes over a broken friendship: "Mama, she won't play with me!" Mother nudged us on the way to reconciliation: "Invite her over for milk and cookies!" So does our Mother-God lead us down the lane to forgiveness and restored friendship, if we listen to her "nudgings." And the restoration brings empowerment. All these gifts are the bequest of our Mothering God, the fruits of Mother-touch, which shared, miraculously multiply a thousand-fold. It is like the seed planted in the good soil which brings forth a hundred-fold.

(Pat Lehrer, media specialist)

Questions for Personal Reflection or Group Discussion

1. Take the popular song and change the pronoun: "She's got the whole world in Her hands." Is the concept of God having the world in *Her* hands a fitting one? How does this concept relate to the idea of God's maternal touch?

2. In Mary's prayer we see the powerful hands of God crushing the enemy and lifting up the afflicted ones. Consider these lines from the Magnificat (Luke 1:52-53 *NRSV*. The word *God* is substituted for the masculine pronoun *he* in these verses.)

"God has shown strength with God's arm;
God has scattered the proud;
   in the thoughts of their hearts
God has brought down the powerful
   from their thrones,
     and lifted up the lowly;
God has filled the hungry with good things,
     and sent the rich away empty."

Does this paradox in these lines disturb you? Are the two ideas (crushing the enemy and tenderly raising up the defenseless; filling the hungry and sending the rich away empty) contradictory? Is this a dualistic concept of God, or is it part of the complexity of our God who is always "more than" any image can project?

3. In the above passage we recalled Jesus rescuing Peter at sea. Have you ever been "at sea"? Has Mother-God been your rescuer? How? Describe. How have you been a rescuer to others? If you have not been, can you think of ways that you might be?

4. The human hand wields a great deal of power; for example, when we think of a surgeon performing a delicate and complex operation. In the church the laying on of hands at confirmation is a symbol that the power of God informs us. In what other ways do hands suggest power—human and godly—to you? Have you experienced Mother-God's power touching, changing, transforming your life? others? the world?

Prayer Suggestions

1. Begin by centering yourself. Recall the lyrics of the hymn, "I will bear you up on eagle's wings." Imagine yourself being swept up and rescued by an eagle. What was the eagle's touch like? In the same song, the lyrics say that you will be held in the palm of God's hand. Is there a sense of security in being held in God's hand? Is being held in the Mother eagle's wings different from being held in God's palm? Share your response with Mother-God. Sing or say the lyrics of this hymn over and over (like a mantra) to remind you of Mother-God's protective care for you—no matter what danger or difficulty you may face.

2. Recall the most poignant experiences in which God personally touched you. Have you felt *Her* touch most in the bad times or in the good. Offer thanks for God's intervention in the happenings of your life.

3. It is a motherly trait to give special and tender attention to the most helpless, deficient and needy of the family. The retarded child or cerebral palsied child seems to be the recipients of a largess of mother-love. Take a few moments to reflect on this thought. Is this akin to the scriptures' assertion that God "puts down the mighty from their thrones and exalts the lowly?" Does it seem contradictory that people not in the mainstream of social life are the ones most loved by God? How can this be? Have you personally witnessed instances to justify God's Mother-hen love for "Her broken-winged children"? Share your response to these questions with Mother-God.

4. The maternal touch of God is a healing touch. Reflect on people that you know now who are in need of both physical and emotional healing. What ways can you help them in their healing process? In what ways have healers helped you?

5. What obstacles have blocked healing in your life? in the lives of others you know? Talk to your Mother about your worry, anxiety, mistrust etc. Write down the obstacles you have discovered and the way you have overcome these negative emotions and opened yourself to God's healing love.

6. Has your Mother-God suggested to you ways to be reconciled with those with whom you have had altercation? Have you followed or fought Her inner promptings? What changes do you need to make in your life to re-establish a relationship? Share your thoughts and feelings about this with Mother-God.

7. There are innumerable instances of healing performed by Jesus throughout the gospels. Jot down your favorite healing story? Why is it your favorite? Do you see in Jesus maternal, compassionate qualities?

8. Have you met women in whom you felt the tenderness of Mother God's caress or the salvific strength of your Mother's outstretched hands? Recall them by name. Thank God for the way they embody Her tenderness and steadfast love. Does this reflection help you understand better that love of God which is called "unconditional"?

9. Record your feelings, images, thoughts, insights, decisions in a journal, poetry, art, song, dance or in some other creative way.

A Balloon Ride with Sophia

Scripture Image

(Jesus) breathed on them and said to them: "Receive the Holy Spirit."

John 20:22 (*NRSV*)

Nicodemus said to him, 'How can anyone be born after growing old?' 'Can one enter a second time into the mother's womb and be born?' Jesus answered, 'Very truly, I tell you, no one can enter the Kingdom of God without being born of water and spirit. What is born of the flesh is flesh and what is born of the Spirit is spirit. Do not be astonished that I said to you, 'You must be born from above. The wind blows where it chooses, and you hear the sound of it but you do not know where it comes from or where it goes. So it is with everyone who is born of the Spirit.

John 3:4-8 (*NRSV*)

We are a group of faith sharing women from diverse backgrounds. We come together on a regular basis to pray, share and support one another in our lives. All are involved in family, parish work and community work. Five of us are wives and mothers and one is a Missionary Sister of the Sacred Heart.

We named our group *Sophia* because as we journeyed together we recognized and appreciated the gift of wisdom and we discovered the personification of Wisdom as Woman or "*Sophia*." We have been meeting for four years.

"A Balloon ride with *Sophia*" is a shared experience of our meeting. We delight in each other because here is where we meet the Feminine Divine. The picture and idea was created by the artist in our group—Mary Lou.

- Mary Lou is the mother of eight, a nurturer, an artist.
- Pam is mother of one, a nurturer, CCD coordinator in our parish.
- Renee is mother of a blended family of five, a nurturer, first grandmother in the group.
- Maria is the mother of four, a nurturer, a nurse.
- Lynda is the mother of five, a nurturer, a vision person.

- Theresa is a Missionary Sister of the Sacred Heart, a nurturer, nurse, missionary. She come to us as a group spiritual leader.

Questions for Personal Reflection or Group Discussion

1. How did you experience *Sophia* on this balloon ride?

2. Where did *Sophia* take you?

3. What discoveries did you make about self? others? the earth? the cosmos? Did *Sophia* reveal any new challenges or insights that seem significant?

4. How did you experience Jesus in this meditation?

Prayer Suggestions

1. We begin our prayer time with a request to the Holy Spirit. We ask that she fill us with her gift of creativity-because we are about to take an extraordinary journey. We are about to pray with our imagination:

Begin by:

- Relaxing

- Become comfortable

- Sink deeply into your chair

- Breathe deeply

- Bring yourself to prayer

- Welcome the Spirit of God

- Delight in the Breath of the Spirit of *Sophia*

2. Time to leave now! Look over there! A very large basket big enough to climb into. Look up! It is attached to a large balloon—Can you see? The balloon has something written on it—It says "*Sophia.*" Let's climb in.

3. Are you ready? Who is here? What are you bringing with you?

4. Here you go. The balloon seems to want to take you somewhere. Where might *Sophia* take you?

5. Up, up and away. What a sight to behold! How does it feel to be above all that is familiar?

6. Look! There's a figure. Do you see? He seems to be beckoning to you. The balloon alights. You climb out. Jesus meets you. He

enfolds you in his arms in greeting. You feel the love of Jesus permeating your entire being. Jesus tells you He has been looking forward to today—to this meeting. *Sophia* has brought you to Him. He looks deeply into your eyes and asks you "What is on your heart today?"

7. Spend time sharing your thoughts and feelings with Jesus.

8. Then—listen to Jesus with all your heart and be filled.

9. It is now time for *Sophia* to take you back. Climb into the basket. Jesus blows His breath into *Sophia*. She ascends. The journey passes quickly. Was it a dream? I open my eyes and look into yours and delight to see Jesus again. Record your feelings, images, thoughts, insights, decisions in a journal, poetry, art, song, dance or in some other creative way.

Epiphany

Feast of God "showing Herself"

Oh, how different my understanding of Revelation!

How do you come to me?

In Molly, my dog who curls around at my feet.

Through my beautiful blue great heron who preens herself
    and sits at my request,

Who comes out into the field with her companion as I ask.

In that wonderful honking Canadian goose who displays for me
with pride her new springtime brood.

In Wood duck paddling the pond, little ones astring behind.

In Mother Earth agonizing as she cries and moans through me
when I touch her.

O Gifts of the sea—my shells—how I treasure you and want to
know your story. You lived immersed in saline ocean. You know
that wonder-filled watery womb. You are, yourselves, the empty
wombs of a last generation of scallops, snails and clams.

Tell me about it. Let me descend with you into the ocean's
depths.

Imbibe the brilliance of iridescent fish, the multiplicity of life,
the flow of energy, from which I come, from whence the scientists
say all came.

Divine Osprey Who left me the egg—I cannot forget you.

Ah, this is the true me,

Who sees You clearly in Your birthed creation.

I find you now, The Divine Feminine revealing Your beauty, in
creation.

Who understands it? Who needs to? It is.

(Nancy M. Healy S.F.C.C., M.A.; Director of The Well Retreat
Center, Smithfield, Virginia)

Questions for Personal Reflection or Group Discussion

1. How does the Feminine Divine reveal Her beauty in creation?

2. What impact does the "Epiphany" of the Feminine Divine
have on you? your relationships? the earth? the cosmos?

3. How does this "Epiphany" affect political, economic, social and religious systems?

4. What can you do to delight more fully in the Feminine Divine present in creation? present in yourself?

Prayer Suggestions

1. Go out into the wonder-full Creation. (If weather or circumstances do not permit, use the "magic carpet" of your imagining—it's always available and it "works"!

2. Breathe deeply of the very Presence of the Feminine Divine. As you breathe out, let go slowly of concerns, responsibilities, duties, stresses in your life. Relax and be. Sit in that receptive feminine mode, willing to receive.

3. Let an image of an animal or a plant come to you. (rock, tree, water, rabbit, squirrel, or. . . .). Welcome it. Just be with it. Delight in it. Let the Feminine Divine guide you. Just be with it in the manner of two old people who know one another so well that they need do nothing else but sit together.

4. When you're ready, consider how it felt to be with the image, animal, plant etc. Why do you think *this* image came to you at this time? What does it have to teach you? Does it guide you to any action in inner and or/ outer world?

5. Journal your thoughts, feelings and insights.

6. Honor the image by creating in poetry or painting or clay or . . . any way you choose. Remember the product matters *not at all*. The process of honoring the symbol or image is everything.

7. Put it in a place of honor.

8. Remember it whenever you need or desire.

9. In the weeks, months, years which follow, you may wish to repeat this exercise. If you do so, record your feelings, images, thoughts, insights, decisions in a journal, poetry, art, song, dance or in some other creative way.

The One Who Answers When I Call

In the language of one African tribe the word for 'God' translates: "the one who answers when I call." For Karl Rahner, God is "always already there." In other words, God anticipates every need, comprehends the depth and intricacy of every emotional and psychological deficit and is always, always, about "wholling us!"

For me this is a "mama" experience of God. My mother was the one person in my life who was "always already there." She was the "one who answered whenever I called." The first thing my brother and I did as flung open the kitchen door after school each day was to cry out: "Mama!" From somewhere within the womb of our home would come the reassuring: "Here I am, honey!"

We needed nothing more. We didn't even need to find her. All our needs were satisfied in the consolation that the person who could solve everything for us was already there and ready.

Scripture doesn't tell us a lot about Mary, but I believe it shows us this ever-present, ever-ready motherliness in Jesus' mother. She is always there for him and with him in the big moments of his life; even at those devastating times of his ultimate rejection and execution. She is also there for John, at the foot of the Cross, and she is there for all Jesus' fair weather followers in their upper-room shame. The Book of Acts places her with them in that Upper Room—so comforting for us to know—that she who could easily point the finger or hold the grudge is so far from that and anything else accusatory. She displays only a compassionate embrace of the weakened, humbled, shame-filled, erstwhile friends of her Son. The tradition of the Church sees her, again and again, associating, down the years, down the generations, even with the so-so followers of the original, fickle followers. Her very motherly presence and embrace seems to be a healing balm capable of changing fickleness into fortitude; and personal ambition into selfless oblation.

In this tenacious, fortitudinal motherly presence, Mary and my own mother mirror for me the maternal God who in my own life-experiences of need has proven, again and again, to be always already there, with an answer to my every call.

(Regina Madonna Oliver S.S.C., M.A. M.T.S., Pastoral Associate at Fort Belvoir Chapel, Alexandria, Virginia.)

Questions for Personal Reflection or Group Discussion

1. Do you have recollections of an ever-ready maternal presence in your life—either that of your birth mother, or of your grandmother, foster mother, or other female whose bonding with you involved total commitment? List some. Share some.

2. Is it enough for you, sometimes, just to hear a reassuring voice say: "I'm here for you." Enough so that you do not even need to seek the person out? Have you thought of that as symbolic of the way God is with you?

3. When you are feeling "erstwhile" and "fickle" about your responses to God's outreaching for a relationship with you, does it help you to think about Mary as a reflection of God's unconditional and compassionate love, which understands, and reaches out, even in the face of truculence, to heal?

4. When you think of God in terms of "Mother" and of Mary as, par excellence, a model or image of that motherliness in God, does that help you to a more mature experience of Mary in your Christian life?

Prayer Suggestions

1. Settle into an aura of silence and wonder that God's love is so personal for you, and so unaffected by your petty peccadillos; as to seek you out persistently and to refuse to be put off by your inattentiveness. Say as your mantra, *"Ammah! Ammah!* Thank you for never giving up on me!"

2. What is the inner core of your being crying out to out Amah-God at this moment? What is your primary heart's longing? Let it surface, and cry it out to *Ammah.* Hear Her assure you that She is there for you.

3. What are the needs of your sisters and brothers in this lifewalk? Especially the needs of the ones who have not yet learned to cry them out for themselves? Cry them out to *Ammah* for your sisters and brothers.

4. Think of the human mother-figure in your life—the one who most embodied those characteristics of unconditional love for you. Think of that person's needs. Thank *Ammah* for that person; and intercede to *Ammah*-God for her needs.

5. Reflect on Mary's presence in the stories of Scripture when Jesus needs her: at his birth; at his Presentation in the Temple; at his Bar-Mitzvah in the Temple in Jerusalem—his 12-year-old

coming to 'manhood'; at their friends' wedding in Cana; during his street-preaching, when people are saying he is 'out-of-his-head; on the Via Dolorosa; at the foot of the cross in Golgotha; with his followers in the Upper Room. Thank Mary for being "always there" for him. Thank Mary for the way she reflects the motherliness of our God.

6. Reflect on how Mary and your mother-figure are alike in this trait of being ready to answer your call, and being there for you at all times. Can you see some of these characteristics in your own life and interaction with others? Could this reflection help you in being a clearer mirror of the motherliness of God as you interact with others? Your spouse? Your children? Your friends, Those you minister to in your job? etc.

7. Are there other people in your life who at some time have demonstrated to you this kind of tenacious, consistent love? List them in your mind; and enjoy recalling their love for you.

8. Share with *Ammah*-God how you want to reflect Her in your life of loving others.

9. Record your feelings, images, thoughts, insights, decisions in a journal, poetry, art, song, dance or in some other creative way.

Women: Images of the Feminine Divine

> Womb of Creation,
>> Shekinah, She-Who-Dwells Within
>>> God, the breasted One
>>>> Woman Mentor
>>>>> *Sophia*, Holy Wisdom

Help women to delight in their identity as *imago Dei* (images of God).

> Angry Woman Preacher
>> Liberator of the Oppressed
>>> Welcoming Hostess
>>>> Washerwoman God
>>>>> Seamstress Elegant

Transform patriarchal structures and sexist attitudes that prevent us from acknowledging women as *imago Dei*.

> Jesus-*Sophia*, the Crucified One
>> Mother Jesus, birthing the world
>>> Merciful Mother Jesus,
>>>> Jesus-*Sophia*, Healer of our Stress
>>>>> Jesus, Mirror of *Sophia*

Reveal your saving power through women, *imago Dei*.

> Grandmother,
>> Sister,
>>> Friend,
>>>> Lover,
>>>>> Companion

Embrace us as Woman through women, *imago Dei*.

(Bridget Mary Meehan S.S.C., D. Min.)

Questions for Personal Reflection or Group Discussion

1. Do you believe that women are created in the image of God (*imago Dei*)? What implications does this belief have on your perceptions of women's roles today? (in work? society? church? politics? medicine? law? science? etc.)

2. Does the church proclaim that women are created in the image of God? What difference does this belief make in its doctrines? worship? practices? policies?

3. How do you feel about the church's position on the role of women in the church? Are women today reshaping the church's attitudes toward women? What are your hopes for the future of women in ministry in the church?

4. Could you describe your experience of one or more of the images of the Feminine Divine in this litany?

Prayer Suggestions

1. Breathe slowly and consciously. Relax your body from the top of your head to the soles of your feet. With your eyes closed and your body relaxed, journey to your center where the Feminine Divine dwells within you. Repeat slowly the word "*Sophia*" (or your favorite name for the Feminine Divine) as you breathe in and as you breathe out. Then, simply, delight in Her presence for several minutes.

2. Open your eyes and pray the Litany to the Feminine Divine.

3. Choose one or several of the images in this litany for prayerful reflection. As you reflect on these images, how do you feel? Did one image appeal to you more than others? Why?

4. Select one image from this litany that touches you. Pray it over and over again, allowing it to sink into the depths of your being. As you do so, open yourself to an intimate encounter with the Feminine Divine. What did you discover about yourself as *imago Dei* from this encounter? Did you find any hidden treasures, places of new life, dynamic energy stirring within you?

5. Write a description of any images that emerge from this prayer experience or draw a picture of them. Be aware of any thoughts, feelings, insights, that you experience as you do so.

6. Pray this litany again for all women, reflections of the *imago Dei*. As you do so, be attentive to any images, thoughts, feelings or insights that emerge. Share these with the Feminine Divine.

7. Be aware of yourself as *imago Dei*. What implications does this understanding have in how you see yourself as a woman? as a man? on your relationships? your work? What implications does this understanding have on how you view the role of women in society? church? politics? Share your insights with the Feminine Divine. Listen to Her response.

8. Reflect on the church's belief that women are created in the image of God. Be aware of how you feel about the church's position on the role of women in the church? Ask the Feminine Divine

to transform patriarchal structures and sexist attitudes that keep us as a church from acting on our belief that women are *imago Dei*.

9. Record your feelings, images, thoughts, insights, decisions in a journal, poetry, art, song, dance or in some other creative way.

Resource Suggestions for Delighting in the Feminine Divine

Bynum, Caroline Walker. *Jesus As Mother* (Berkeley: California, University of California Press, 1982). This book is a collection of scholarly essays presenting some important insights into medieval spirituality. Caroline Walker Bynum gives interesting data on the use of feminine imagery in Medieval piety. Her research introduces us to men and women during this time addressing Jesus as mother Included are excellent footnotes referring to other sources of recent works on the theme of mother Jesus in the Middle Ages.

Cady, Susan, Marian Ronan and Hal Taussig. *Wisdom's Feast* (San Francisco: Harper & Row, 1989). This outstanding book introduces *Sophia's* importance in the Christian tradition and presents her as mother, creator, teacher, wisdom. This is a unique book, one that introduces *Sophia* in powerful ritual settings. Included also are creative exercises, innovative liturgies, challenging sermons, comprehensive study guides and beautiful meditations for individuals and groups interested in exploring the female image of God—*Sophia*, holy "wisdom." Ideal for scripture study and women's groups especially appropriate for ecumenical settings. The section that I found most fascinating was the one describing *Sophia's* relationship with Jesus.

Froehle, Virginia Ann. *Called Into Her Presence* (Notre Dame: Indiana, Ave Maria Press, 1992). A wonderful, gentle introduction to praying with feminine images of God. In this book Virginia Froehle provides the reader with a collection of exercises, experiences and celebration for personal and group prayer. Perfect for retreats and days of recollection. She is also the author of a successful audio cassette program—*In Her Presence: Prayer Experiences Exploring Feminine Images of God* (St. Anthony Messenger Press)

Johnson, Elizabeth A. *She Who Is* (New York: Crossroad, 1992). In this book Elizabeth Johnson does an outstanding job of engaging the classical Christian doctrine of God in a dialogue with feminist theology. *She Who Is* is imaginative and playful while at the same time providing a brilliant and powerful analyses of the doctrine of God, trinitarian theology, Spirit Christology, feminist theology and women's experience.

McFague, Sallie. *Models of God* (Philadelphia: Fortress Press, 1987). *Models of God* is well-written systematic theology that challenges the reader to think creatively and imaginatively about the appropriateness of Christian images of God and their implications for the relationship between God and the world. In this provocative book, Sally McFague presents several new models of God for an ecological, nuclear age: God as Mother, God as Lover, God as Friend.

Meehan, Bridget Mary. *Exploring the Feminine Face of God* (Kansas City: Sheed & Ward, 1991). *Exploring the Feminine Face of God* presents new ways for women and men to pray with feminine images of God within the Christian tradition in Scripture, the mystics and contemporary writings. After each reflection a series of guided prayer experiences is provided to help the reader to enter into a prayerful encounter with the image. This book helps individuals and small faith sharing groups to expand their images of God, to heal hurts in their mother-relationship, to embrace their feminine side, and to experience God's feminine presence in their lives. Four experiences of praying with feminine images are available on videotape: *Exploring the Feminine Face of God* (Kansas City: Sheed & Ward).

Rae, Eleanor, and Marie-Daly, Bernice. *Created In Her Image* (New York: Crossroad, 1990). *Created In Her Image* presents the need for a system of symbols and images that affirm the dignity of women. Rooted in the conviction that it is essential for humanity to affirm the feminine virtues of birthing, nurture, responsibility, integrity in order to survive in our contemporary world, Rae and Marie-Daly introduce a gender free model of the Judeo-Christian tradition that embraces political, social and ecological justice that foster the survival of the earth and humankind. I found their eco-feminist critique especially challenging.

Craighead, Meinrad. *The Mother's Songs* (New York: Paulist Press, 1986). A beautiful, evocative book of paintings of God the Mother that has the power, I believe, to bring forth new images, feelings, and insights into our relationship with the Feminine Divine dwelling in the depths of our being. Each picture in the book tells a story, from Meinrad's life experiences. "My personal vision of God the Mother," comments Craighead in her introduction, "incarnated in my mother and her mother, gave me from childhood, the clearest certainty of woman as the truer image of Divine Spirit."

Fulmer, Colleen. *Cry of Ramah* (Albany, California: Loretto Spirituality Network, [725 Calhoun Street, 94709] 1990). An audio tape and book of songs with dances by Martha Ann Kirk that celebrate women's creative imagination. Ideal for women's prayer services.

Gjerding, Iben, and Katherine Kinnamon, eds. *Women's Prayer Services* (Mystic, Connecticut: Twenty-Third Publications, 1983). A provocative attempt to introduce feminine images of God in prayer, calls to worship, reflections, psalms, benedictions, litanies etc. that expands our understanding of the mystery of God. An excellent resource for women's celebrations in ecumenical settings.

Schneiders, Sandra. *Women and The Word* (New York: Paulist, 1986). This book focuses on the gender of God in the New Testament and presents a concise overview of the following topics: the types of language about God in the Hebrew Scriptures; metaphors for God in the Hebrew Scriptures; Jesus' experience and presentation of God; the significance of the maleness of Jesus and the spirituality of women and men in relation to a male Savior.

Sleevi, Mary Lou. *Women of the Word* (Notre Dame: Ave Maria Press, 1989). This award-winning artistic book features some of the most powerful paintings of Biblical women that I have seen. The text reveals rich glimpses and insights into the encounter of each woman with the Divine. *Women of the Word*, a book of prayerful reflections, is perfect for individual and group use.

Swidler, Leonard. *Biblical Affirmations of Woman* (Philadelphia: Westminster Press, 1979). A comprehensive, well-documented commentary on what the Bible teaches about women. Included are topics, such as: God a loving Mother; The Holy Spirit is a Woman; and Feminine Imagery of God in the Biblical and Post-biblical Period. This scholarly resource is an excellent reference tool for clarifying biblical understandings of feminine images of God as well as for discovering positive perspectives on women in the Bible.

Winter, Miriam Therese. *Woman Prayer Woman Song* (Oak Park, Illinois: Meyer Stone Books, 1987). *Woman Prayer Woman Song* provides the reader with a rich collection of ritual resources featuring feminine biblical images, new songs, new celebrations appropriate for worship. Through creation rituals we awaken to the feminine in the cosmos as we encounter *"El Shaddai,"* often translated "the breasted one." Included also in this book are liberation ritual which free the feminine in worship and transformation rituals which incorporate the present and past by journeying from death to life "in every woman's here and now." The prefaces, liturgies and songs are a wonderful resource for renewing the Christian tradition through women's experience.

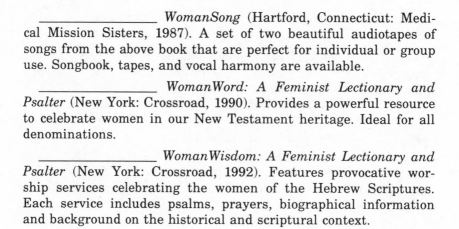

_____ *WomanSong* (Hartford, Connecticut: Medical Mission Sisters, 1987). A set of two beautiful audiotapes of songs from the above book that are perfect for individual or group use. Songbook, tapes, and vocal harmony are available.

_____ *WomanWord: A Feminist Lectionary and Psalter* (New York: Crossroad, 1990). Provides a powerful resource to celebrate women in our New Testament heritage. Ideal for all denominations.

_____ *WomanWisdom: A Feminist Lectionary and Psalter* (New York: Crossroad, 1992). Features provocative worship services celebrating the women of the Hebrew Scriptures. Each service includes psalms, prayers, biographical information and background on the historical and scriptural context.